MW01203917

MUSTARD
EVERY
MONDAY

From Secluded Convent

to

International Adventure

MEMOIR

ANNE FANGMAN

Publishing-Partners

Publishing-Partners
Port Townsend, WA 98368
www.Publishing-Partners.com

10 9 8 7 6 5 4 3 2 1
Printed in the United States of America
Library of Congress Control Number: 2016930768
ISBN: 978-0-9862830-7-9
eISBN: 978-0-9862830-8-6

Cover design: Marcia Breece
Typography: Marcia Breece
eBook: Marcia Breece

Table of Contents

Dad, Mom,
Anne, Bruce, Mary Jo
1940

❦ PROLOGUE ❦

One thing about growing up Catholic, it can mess up your mind. In 1957, I convinced myself I should enter a convent. This kind of "message from God" was not unusual for an eighteen-year-old Catholic girl in Omaha, Nebraska. The enthusiasm for going into religious life was contagious. Anybody who was anybody was entering the convent in those days: the girl who had the lead in the spring play, the class president, and the homecoming queen candidate for Prep (the local boys' Catholic school). Of course, a few shy, less-than-popular girls went but with less notice. I was not one of the super popular girls but I held my own among the moderately popular.

Omaha was and, as far as I can tell, still is a very Catholic, Midwestern, conservative city. People liked Ike, our 34th president. Men and women had clearly defined roles and sex education in schools was non-existent. Neither the hippie movement nor the womens' movement had yet to become part of everyday conversation. TV was a novelty. The choices were simple for young girls: they could be teachers, nurses, or secretaries before becoming wives and mothers (in that order, mind you). That was about it. It never once dawned on me that I could explore the big, bad world on my own.

To this day, though, I can't put my finger on any single motive for my entering a convent, though some reasons come to mind. I had been under the influence of the Sisters of Mercy for twelve years and, coming from a classically dysfunctional family, I had developed a need to be the perfect daughter. My parents, like many Catholic parents, thought my decision to serve in the religious life was a gift, a blessing on our family that God had chosen one of their children. I had developed a normal teenage need to be noticed and belong, so I chose the most dramatic way available to me. I entered a convent. My young brain had not yet matured in the areas governing rational thought or impulsive behavior. I jumped right in without much deep thinking.

What I *really* wanted was to be a nurse, fall in love with a handsome doctor, and have a family. I didn't think that was asking too much. *Sue Barton, Student Nurse* books were saying that sort of life could happen. I, however, was so strongly influenced by the Catholic Church that I couldn't ignore the voices whispering in my mind that I should become a Sister of Mercy. The priest who led our senior High School retreat, a three-day time of spirituality and silence, told us we would not be happy if we ignored the call to religious life. That thought grabbed me by the throat. Ignoring God would have been like not answering the door when you know George Clooney is standing outside. I decided I'd better check it out. I was afraid *not* to check it out. I figured I could always decide to leave, a plan which proved to be *much* easier said than done. I had no way of knowing it would take me more than eight years to figure out the difference between religion and spirituality. When the day finally came that I walked away from years of conditioning, it was the happiest day of my life.

CRAZY BARB

The person who evolved into my best buddy and biggest influence through grade school, high school, and the convent was Barb. In fifth grade, she was the new kid in class. At first we didn't like each other and either ignored or glared to communicate our feelings. For some unknown reason, in the middle of the school year, our teacher decided to assign seats in alphabetical order. So there we were, the two of us, stuck with Barbie sitting behind Annie. Hostilities began to melt when we discovered our birthdays were on the same day; somehow, that felt special, suggesting some bond between us. By eighth grade we were best buddies and known for being fun and trouble.

High school cemented our friendship. Barb lived two blocks from me and we would walk the mile from school and stand talking on the corner where our paths parted. Then we would call each other as soon as we got home. Dad would tease, "What in heaven's name do you two still have to talk about?" When we had sleepovers, it was always at Barb's much quieter home. She was an only child and had a lovely bedroom all to herself. I, on the other hand, shared a bedroom with my sister, Marty, who was eight years younger and a tomboy. She wore cowboy outfits and played with the neighbor boys. She would come home all sweaty, sling

Marty with her sidekick, Linda

her gun and holster on the bedroom door knob, drop her cowboy hat on the nice pink bedspread, and hang her dirty chaps in the closet right next to my nice, clean clothes. It was not an arrangement conducive to my adolescent need for privacy or being pretty.

Senior year was a time to get ready for the career we had chosen. Because I wanted to be a nurse, I was advised to take Latin and math classes. Barb wasn't sure what she wanted to do after high school so she took fun classes like home economics and typing. I didn't need home economics; I had been cooking and sewing at home for years. One Christmas I even made pajamas for my brothers, Bruce (three years older) and Paul (three years younger). I doubt they were ever worn. Their "Gee, thanks, Anne," clearly lacked enthusiasm. Dad, on the other hand, wore the brown corduroy shirt I made for him until it was so threadbare Mom insisted he get rid of it. He always made sure I knew he appreciated anything I did for him, including periodically making pancakes.

Since I was such an expert at making pajamas, one spring evening Barb asked me to help her finish a pair due for her home economics class the next morning. We sat in her bedroom till 1:30 A.M. while I sewed and she read poems to me out of *Good Housekeeping magazine.* I think I put the sleeves in backwards or the back in frontward. The next morning, even though I had dragged her out of bed, paced while she dressed, and rushed us to school, I was the only one marked tardy! She had a knack for not getting caught. She could look innocent. Not me. I looked guilty.

The reason Barb had not finished the pajama project was because we had spent the earlier part of the evening pulling a prank on Dee, a buddy of ours. She had made the mistake of telling us she was going to a performance of chamber music with a guy we thought was dorky. Hmmmm. We needed to do something about this. We donned Bermuda shorts, high heeled shoes with bobby sox (considered a strange combination at the time), and thick rimless glasses we found in a junk drawer. As we drove up to her house, we realized we had timed our arrival perfectly. Her date had just arrived. As I stepped out of the car, I donned the thick glasses and tripped up the steps to the front door. We greeted Dee with an exaggerated high society affect.

"Dahling, aren't you going to ask your two best friends in to say hello?"

"OK, guys, you look weird; what are you up to now?"

"My dear, we thought you were going to the Book-of-the-Month-Club meeting with us."

At that point she rolled her eyes and let us in. Her Old World parents sat on the sofa in amazed silence. Just as we were being introduced to The Dork, a perfectly timed alarm clock went off in Barb's purse. Using all the dramatic talent she possessed, which was considerable, she pulled a bottle of cough syrup and a huge wooden spoon out of her purse. "Time to take my medicine!" she chirped. To keep a straight face, I turned away, tripped over the coffee table, and dislodged my coke-bottle glasses. We looked like a skit from a Lucille Ball show. By the time Barb and I could look at each other again, we found ourselves alone with the still-silent parents. "Hi. Nice to see you again." Silence. "Um, bye now. Have a nice evening." Silence. Wave. Dee later laughed with us about the incident and the three of us, oddly matched as we were, stayed good friends and became known as The Three Musketeers.

Every once in a while, Barb would ask me why I called her Crazy Barb. I said I didn't know; she just was. Not crazy-crazy, just zany-crazy. When pressed, I could come up with a lot of examples, like the time we overslept *again* after another slumber party at her house and were late for Mass. Barb got the bright idea we could make it on time by rolling up our pajama legs (definitely not approved church attire) and throwing on long raincoats. The outfit worked fine until we stood in line for Holy Communion. Her familiar giggle from behind stopped me in my tracks. "Annie, your pajama leg just fell down! Everyone is looking at you!" There was no way to stifle ourselves so we darted for the side door, snorting and tripping.

"You looked so silly!"

"Well, it was all your idea, you know."

"Who, me?"

"Yes, you."

"Let's go for doughnuts."

In those days Barb and I didn't talk about anything serious, so I had no idea she was thinking of entering the convent. I assumed she would get married. She always had a boyfriend around. She was cute, wore lots of new clothes, and had long hair she could put into a Debbie Reynolds-type ponytail. I had pimples, made my own clothes, and had hair that wouldn't go into anything. Toward the end of our senior year, Barb surprised me by saying she had thought of entering a convent since she was a little girl. She used to dress up in black with white around her face pretending to be a Nun. Me, I hadn't given it much thought until the spiritual retreat during my senior year when I decided to give it a try. I was fearful of my life not working if I passed up a call from God. Many years later a friend of mine said, "This is so interesting to me. What made God so powerful for you? I got similar religious indoctrination, but if God had a bull horn and called my name, I would have hidden in a closet till he left." I laugh at it now but I couldn't begin to think that way when I was a teenager. Because life had been so difficult and arbitrary for my parents, I grew up not realizing I had a right to pursue happiness.

Barb and I speculated about others entering the convent with us; we hoped it would be some fun people. Little did we know being surrounded by fun people in a convent would be a hindrance instead of a help. We wrote the exact same letters to Mother Provincial asking permission to enter the Sisters of Mercy. We mailed them the same day from the same mailbox. We didn't want anyone to know we had written the letters together, however, so we wrote on different colored stationary. Fooled them! I was thrilled my best friend would be in the convent with me. We had our own special secret and when we were alone we would teasingly address each other with, "Yes, Sister Barbara" and "Thank you, Sister Anne." We speculated about whether Nuns wore bras, what they did all day, and how they could wear all that starch and wool in the summer. Our biggest question was: Do we have to shave our heads? We would find out soon enough.

About the only information we had on the history of the Sisters of Mercy in 1957 was a summary in the back of a Sisters of Mercy calendar:

Mother McAuley, Foundress of the Sisters of Mercy, was born on the Feast of St. Michael, September 29, 1778. From her youth, Catherine cherished a love of God's poor; as a wealthy lady in Irish society, she established a house of Mercy in Dublin. She was assisted in this work by a group of women who shared her desire to serve God in his suffering humanity.

Catherine McAuley soon realized that this work had outgrown its inception, and, at the direction of Archbishop Daniel Murray, made plans to incorporate her band of workers into a new Religious Congregation. Thus, on December 12, 1831, Sister Catherine pronounced her Religious Vows and founded the Sisters of Mercy. Only ten short years later, on June 6, 1841, the Rules and Constitutions were confirmed by Pope Gregory XVI. In this same year, on November 11, Mother McAuley died.

Today, the Sisters of Mercy number over 24,000. Just as Christ's love extends to all the members of His Mystical Body, so the charity of the Sisters of Mercy reaches out to the poor, sick and ignorant on every continent in the world.

Okay, nothing new there. We'd been hearing about Mother McAuley for years. I respected her devotion to the poor, but I was never super-impressed by her need to live her life for them. Every year the seniors at Mercy High School would put on a big production for Mercy Day. I had the Oscar-worthy role of the Blessed Virgin Mary. It consisted of standing like a statue during the closing scene while trying to keep my hands from shaking.

Next page: Bruce, Anne, Mary Jo, Paul in swing, 1945

❧ FAMILY ❧

The evening I told Mom and Dad about my decision to enter the convent, I found them reading the evening paper in their usual places on either end of the sofa. I wanted them to be happy about my decision. Being Catholic was very important to them, and they were spending hard-earned money sending us kids to Catholic schools. My decision surprised them. They could have talked me out of it with very little effort but they were not good at discussing feelings or thoughts with their children. Instead, Dad hugged me and did his usual speaking for both of them, "We're very proud of you, Anne. We always knew God had saved you for something special. Now we know what it is." I felt pleased I was fulfilling what I thought was his wish. Years later, my sister, Marty, told me he grieved my decision and the hole it left in his life. I was Daddy's girl and I missed him every bit as much as he missed me.

Most of the childhood memories I cherish have Dad in the picture: riding my new bicycle, learning to swim, raking leaves, and playing with Christmas toys. He was very funny and frequently made me laugh. I know I developed my sense of humor from him.

He was also very gracious and **elegant and** I think of him as a combination of Fred Astaire, George Burns, and Dick Van Dyke. Dad was the nurturing parent, and he often played the role of both father and mother. None of us kids could get up in the middle of the night without him hearing us and getting up to ask if we were O.K. When I was in high school several of my girlfriends had crushes on him. Whenever a group of us piled in a car to go somewhere, I would be the last one picked up and first one taken home so everyone could see Dad when he came out to the car to say hi or good-bye. I was so proud of him. He was very handsome and charming. He had a way of remembering details and would ask how a girl's vacation was or how a sick mother was doing. Even though he was an insurance salesman he wasn't good at names. I took after him on that. One evening as a date was about to arrive, I realized I couldn't remember his name. "Daaaaaaad, what am I going to do? This is embarrassing!" He laughed and told me to stay up in my room while he answered the door, introduced himself, and then came upstairs to tell me my date's name. I *always* felt loved by Dad.

My memories of Mom are not as vivid or as loving. She was almost movie star beautiful and very charming with a good sense of color and dress. But she never seemed happy. When I would come through the back door after school she was always home but it felt as if nobody was there. She had very little to say, usually keeping busy with housework. Sometimes she would blurt out sarcastic statements to me in front of Dad: "Men are a lot of trouble." "Having children is not as wonderful as you think it is." I learned to keep my thoughts to myself but swore if I ever got married and had children I would never say things like that. I don't remember her ever hugging or holding me and we certainly did not have Mother-daughter talks. I was already a 34B when I went without her to buy my first bra.

⌒

I can understand Dad thinking I was saved for something special. I almost died when I was six years old from measles encephalitis. Instead of the ordinary childhood virus that led to breaking out in spots all over my body, the infection went to my brain causing a coma. Mom and Dad said later they knew I was sick when I refused an ice cream cone. By the time Dad had carried me into the hospital I was limp as a rag doll and was not expected to live through the night. My parents were told, if I did live, I would need to learn to walk and talk all over again. The only memory I have of that night was a sort of out-of-body-experience, looking down on the people hovering over me as I lay on a gurney and feeling the need to go back into my body. The pediatrician worked through the night replacing my blood with transfusions. Medicine had little else to offer in 1945 as antibiotics were too new to be commonly used. Our parish priest administered the Sacraments for the Dying and then Mom and Dad went home to get some rest. They were awakened the next morning by a phone call from an excited nurse. "She is going to be all right! When I tried to brush her hair, she told me to go jump in the lake!" Amazingly, I recovered completely and did not need to re-learn any motor skills.

I don't remember how long I was in the hospital. As a child, it felt like a long, long time, but when I questioned Dad later, he said, "Oh, I think it was a couple of weeks." Those weeks were terribly lonely. I was kept in isolation because I was considered infectious. My parents had been instructed to burn all my toys and clothes. I couldn't understand why Mom and Dad had to stay outside the hospital ward and wave at me through a small window in the door. Why couldn't they come in and give me a hug? I felt fine. Why couldn't I go home? Why did I have to stay in bed? The nurses always seemed in a hurry, except one.

I have no memory of her name but clearly remember her sitting on the bed, shoulder to shoulder, reading bedtime stories. When she left I would cry and hug the one teddy bear I had been allowed to keep. I decided when I grew up I wanted to be a nurse just like her. Other things stayed in my memory, like the lonesome whistle of a train at night. For years I would feel like crying when I heard that sound. I also remembered dreams of falling off a bridge near my home and waking up to breakfasts of prunes and oatmeal. The trauma of that illness seared many details in my mind.

When I came home, I was confined to my bed for several months because any little excitement would cause me to have a grand mal seizure. I spent those months gazing out the bedroom window at the apple tree in bloom, listening to the birds sing, and daydreaming. The noises of summer drifted into my room, and I ached to join the neighbor kids playing or my family having dinner downstairs.

My special time was in the evening when the family would kneel around my bed for night prayers. My brother, Bruce, was three years older than I; my sister, Mary Jo, was fifteen months older and brother, Paul, was three years younger. (Baby sister, Marty, was not on the scene yet.) We God-blessed everybody: Grandma, Grandpa, Nana, the neighbor's dog, friends, and each other. Life seemed much more serious to me after I was sick; on some level I realized how fragile my body could be. Right before having a seizure, I would get a sensation, an aura, of tingling on my tongue and run to find Mom or Dad. I wouldn't remember anything else about the seizures. Their unpredictability motivated me to be a good girl and keep quiet like I was told. I went back to school in the Fall feeling very timid and vulnerable. About a year passed before I could be off my seizure medication and play at recess. My classmates seemed in a world very different from mine and it took most of my grade school years to feel somewhat caught up with them scholastically and socially.

During that year of recovery, I began noticing my sister Mary Jo was no longer able to be the buddy she had been, both physically and mentally. She had been born crippled with clubfeet and dislocated hips. Many of her early years were spent in body casts or leg casts and then corrective shoes. As a toddler, I thought my job was to entertain her and share everything with her. Mom would double-knot the shoelaces on Mary Jo's special orthopedic shoes but I picked away until I accomplished putting them on my feet and clomping around, tripping and giggling for her benefit. She would giggle right back. Mary Jo's surgeries had slowed down her development, and I was quick. As a result, our fifteen-month age difference narrowed and we developed many skills at the same time. We thought we were twins. We held hands, sat squeezed in the same swing, and shared a sandbox. One afternoon, as family folklore goes, Mom looked out the window to see her two toddlers standing in the street buck-naked watching our pee flow down the hill and giggling away. During those years, Mom made most of our clothes and dressed us alike. One time she ordered similar bedroom slippers from the Sears Roebuck catalog. Mary Jo and I didn't like it that one pair was pink and one blue so we each wore a pink slipper and a blue slipper. But by the time we started school she began to slow down mentally and could no longer keep up with me. I felt her loss but didn't understand what was happening.

Mary Jo spent two years in each grade and then the Sisters would simply pass her on. The schools had no one to focus on children with disabilities as they do today. My older brother, Bruce, and I evolved into her guardians. He and I would take turns meeting her in the cloakroom to help with her coat, scarf, and boots and then walk her home. I would watch during recess to make sure the big kids were not teasing her. After second grade she began having convulsions and soon couldn't go to school at all. I felt guilty because her convulsions didn't go away like mine did. As the seizures grew worse, we had difficulty protecting her from falling. When she was fourteen the doctor advised Mom and Dad to put her in the Nebraska State Home for Retarded Children (the culturally incorrect name at the time) in Beatrice, Nebraska. "You have four other beautiful children. Be there for them. Mary Jo won't comprehend what is happening to her." Years later Bruce told me he overheard Mom and Dad discussing that Mary Jo also had an inoperable brain tumor which would explain some of her slow deterioration. I'm sure it never dawned on them to explain that to us kids.

Each time we visited Mary Jo at the state home, she had declined more. She could join the family at a summer picnic in the park or a winter afternoon in a hotel room but her participation in our activities was minimal. She always wore her favorite green dress with a stick figure made of pipe cleaner attached at the shoulder. She appeared happy and able to enjoy our visits, but I couldn't tell if she even knew who I was. Mom and Dad seemed overwhelmed with grief. Mom would cry quietly during the two-hour drive home and Dad would be very silent. Bruce took his big-brother role seriously and made sure we were good kids in the back seat. I missed Mary Jo more than I could understand at the time but kept my emptiness to myself. As kids, we had no encouragement to identify our feelings, let alone verbalize them.

Marty and Dad
1950

Mary Jo, Anne, Bruce
1939

Mary Jo and Anne
in swing, 1941

Mary Jo and Anne in tub,
Paul, Dad,
Bruce standing
1944

Bruce, Mary Jo and Mom
1938

Anne and Barb at Creighton Prep football game, 1956

⤟⤟ HIGH SCHOOL ⤟⤟

My early teen years were lonely. Mom drank heavily and withdrew even more. Womens' drinking was in the closet in those days but, since Mom and Dad often had a drink together before going out to a Friday night dinner (their one luxury), there was always a bottle of bourbon in the house. Several afternoons arriving home from school, I would find Mom still in bed with an empty bottle of Kesslers bourbon on the floor. I had no idea if anyone else in the family knew how much she was drinking. Again, no one talked. Mom seemed so unhappy. She had a husband who loved her and four children who were healthy and needed her. But she couldn't work through her grief for Mary Jo. She seemed to dwell on Mary Jo constantly, crying about her, and giving us the impression we didn't matter. If she had other demons, I was unaware of them. I knew her father abandoned the family when she was three years old, but she never expressed how she felt about him. I think she tried hard to be a good mother when we were young and she must have been exhausted most of the time trying to care for the four of us born within six years. When her relatives came to visit, I often heard them say to her, "Peg, you look so thin," or "Peg, you look so tired." The only times I heard her raise her voice was when she and Dad came home from their Friday night dinners. I would sneak quietly down the stairs wondering what her raised voice was about. Evidently Mom would have had enough to drink to be berating Dad. "I've had YOUR children for you and that's enough!" All I could hear from Dad were quiet murmurs.

Family dinners were the only times the whole family was together and could indulge in bantering and teasing. Even Mom would laugh sometimes. Dad sat at my right and would sneak food off my plate, acting very innocent when I discovered my bread or meat gone. The food bowls were usually at the other end of the table with the boys and the rest of us teased them about having fork marks on our hands if we dared reach for seconds. Paul was the funny one and would regale us with exaggerated tales of his experiences. He and Bruce would play off each other like a comedy team. But when the meals were over they would disappear to be with friends. Dad would go back out to work selling insurance, Mom would vanish to her bedroom, and Marty would go outside to play. I would be left doing the dishes. Then I would retreat to my bedroom feeling very alone and desperately wishing someone would talk to me.

I learned to spend as much time as I could at school and with Barb. She and I got involved in just about every extra-curricular activity that high school offered. We volunteered to stand together on a downtown street corner selling St. Patrick's Day shamrocks for charity. We helped with decorations for junior and senior proms and we tried out for every play and every speech contest.

We were both in our senior spring play, *Quality Street*. Barb had one of the leads, and I played the part of an old maid, Henrietta Thurnbull. Rehearsals ran late one evening so Barb and I opted to stay the night in a school conference room. After we consulted with our parents, one of the Sisters gave us some (properly sewn) pajamas from home economics, blankets and pillows, and a lecture about getting some sleep. O.K. As soon as she left, we started plotting how to sneak into the convent at the far end of the building. We wanted to get a peek at what the Sisters did in the evening. We didn't make it past their front door, though, before getting sent on our way in no uncertain terms. We settled for roaming the school halls in the dark till 2:00 A.M., tripping and giggling. Why we roamed the halls, I don't remember, except that we could.

The two Sisters who were directing the play didn't have much patience with Barb and me and would get irritated when we flubbed lines, which we did frequently. During a break in rehearsals one afternoon, I was showing Barb how to knit using the props from my scene; later onstage I noticed we had dropped a few stitches and I made a face at her. She made a face back. That was the end of that scene. The Sisters gave up on us and said we needed to go to church; it was Good Friday before Easter. Obediently we went to special Good Friday services from 2:00 to 5:00 then Mass at 5:30. After that, we were sick of church and wondered how we would ever manage all the praying we would be expected to do in the convent. We were so hungry we stopped at a diner for a sandwich. Neither one of us had thought about money until the check came.

"I thought you had some."

"Who, me? No way."

"Not to worry, Fearless Barb has a plan."

She casually walked past the other tables picking up enough tips to pay our bill and even leave a tip on our table. As we walked out the door, Barb's only comment was, "I wonder if God was watching."

Since Mercy was an all-girls school, guys from Prep, the boy's high school, filled the male roles in the play. I had a crush on the boy who had the lead. He had a crush on Barb. She didn't give him any encouragement even when they had to rehearse a kissing scene. So he gave up on her and accepted my invitation to the senior prom. I didn't mind playing second fiddle. I just wanted to go to the prom with someone I liked.

I had been dating off and on but never going steady like Barb usually was. The Sisters lectured us constantly about the need to protect our virginity until marriage and to pray to the Blessed Virgin Mary for help. I accepted completely their version of how sex should be avoided and was determined to save myself for marriage. I never wanted to disappoint Mom and Dad by becoming pregnant outside of marriage. The shame of it during that era would have devastated me. One evening, though, I downright embarrassed myself on a double date with a gorgeous basketball player from Prep. We were at a drive-in movie and in the back seat kissing, of course. I was struggling with HOW FAR TO GO, thinking of what the Sisters had drilled into our heads. At that exact moment he whispered, "A penny for your thoughts." Much to my dismay, I blurted, "Oh, I was just thinking of what the Blessed Virgin Mary would do in my place."

"Oh."

No more kisses.

I told Barb about it the next day, moaning and groaning about how stupid that was. Soon blabbermouth Barb had the story all over school.

"Heard you had a hot date last night, Fangman."

"Wanna tell us what the Virgin Mary would do on a date?"

In the spring several of us seniors were chosen to take a one-act play to Kansas City for a national drama convention. It turned out to be a lot of hard work for several days. The last evening of the convention several of us decided to have some fun and not attend the stuffy old banquet. We ditched the Sisters who were our chaperones and snuck into a nearby burlesque theater. We had to sneak in. No one would sell tickets to six high school girls. As we were getting our eyes full of more bare skin than we had ever seen before, the manager (rudely, we thought) told us to leave. He was escorting us from the theater just as the banquet was letting out across the street. The Sisters spotted us. Panic. We dove into a bar on the corner and stood inside the entrance while our eyes adjusted to the dark interior. A guy was onstage imitating Elvis. He and several men in the bar saw us and headed in our direction. To us, they looked like a parade of vultures so we bolted out the door. Laughing and scattering, some of us ran down the street and others darted into the alley and over a fence. Back at the hotel, the Sisters didn't think the whole scene was very funny and lectured us about disgracing the name of Mercy High School. We caught glances of each other and tried to look serious. One of the Sisters asked, "What will your parents think when they find out?" A brave soul blurted out, "Oh, mine will probably laugh." Not the right answer. The Sisters said they would never take Mercy girls to a convention again. Eight years later when my sister, Marty, was at Mercy she was still hearing about our famous episode. Her senior class was not too happy with us since they were still not allowed to go out of town for conventions.

Barb as Postulant
1957

GETTING READY

Preparing to enter a convent is not one of the more exciting things a teenage girl can do. We received instructions from the Motherhouse to bring a dowry check for twenty-five dollars which was a lot of money in 1957. The week before entering, Barb and I put on a style show for our families and friends who wanted to see the latest in Nuns' fashions. Just the underwear covered more of us than our regular summer clothes. First layer: black cotton hose with garter belt, cotton briefs, bra, and t-shirt. We were relieved they wore bras but wondered what purpose a bra would serve under all that clothing. The t-shirts, however, would make a difference by keeping our perspiration from soiling the black wool outer garments which turned out to be a huge challenge to wash. The briefs hit us at the knees and the t-shirts hit below the thighs making us look like 1890s girls at the beach. Our audience chanted, "Put it on, put it on, put it ALL ON!"

The next layer was a long, black, cotton slip with big a pocket accessed through a slit in the habit. We practiced walking in the black oxford shoes which felt like boxes. I had purchased my shoes at Brandies department store on my way home from my job as a hospital nursing assistant. I could tell the shoe salesman didn't know what to make of this young girl trying on old-lady black shoes with a nursing assistant uniform and white hose. I didn't have the heart to tell him, so I just mumbled, "Black is so basic."

⌇

For the last and most stunning layer of our postulant outfit we wore black mid-calf dresses with long sleeves and perfectly sewn pleats. We had such detailed instructions on how to make the dress that we gave up trying to sew them ourselves and asked a neighbor for help. The remainder of the wardrobe included a black wool shawl, black wool mittens, and black galoshes for snow. The aprons could be made of patterned material, as long as the colors were "tasteful." The long, flannel granny nightgowns could be pastel. (I never did conquer wearing long gowns to bed. They bunched up during the night keeping my neck warm while the rest of me froze.) The Mother Superior would complete the outfit the day we entered by giving us a black postulant veil, white plastic cuffs, and a white plastic Peter Pan collar.

We filled the rest of the trunk with the recommended year's supply of toiletry articles: soap, toothpaste, and talcum powder. No perfume. No lace. No frills. Period. Amen. It was a shock to realize how many things they considered frivolous. We brought plenty of everything on the list. We were afraid items issued to us in the convent might have a weird smell or terrible taste.

PATRICK

I was excited to find out four of the guys we had known since first grade were entering the Jesuit seminary shortly before Barb and I were entering the Sisters of Mercy. It felt like much-needed validation for my decision to enter religious life. I was especially relieved one of them was Patrick. With all the crushes on boys I had in grade school and high school, Patrick stayed in my mind. He wasn't especially handsome, cute maybe, but something about him pulled me toward him. In seventh and eighth grades, he and his buddies would start snowball fights with us girls as we trudged the mile home from school. On Saturdays the same group of guys might be nice and carry our ice skates to the rink. We spent the eighth-grade picnic dousing each other with water guns. Patrick didn't give me a whole lot of attention, just enough to keep me encouraged.

Our homes were only a few blocks apart, so Patrick frequently walked past my house on his way to catch a bus. Dad would see him and teasingly say, "Get outside, Anne, your heartthrob is coming down the street." I would rush out the door so I could, casually of course, wave and say "Hi, Patrick." He would be as calm and charming as I was nervous. I felt an attraction to him

I did not experience with anyone else. But, alas, he dated girls from the *other* girls' high school and never asked me out.

The week before entering the Jesuits, as he and I once again stood talking outside my house, he mentioned the date that he and the three others would be leaving for the seminary in Milwaukee. "What we need as our train pulls out of the station is a good, stiff drink." So, Barb and I decided to oblige, true friends that we were. We snitched a bottle of Kesslers bourbon from Mom and Dad's stash and drove downtown to the train station. We attempted to act dignified as we slunk past families and girlfriends on the platform crying over their soon-to-be lost loves.

"You go into the train first, Barb."

"No, you go first."

"This was your idea!"

"MY idea!"

We pushed each other inside and wandered down the aisles searching for the guys. I don't think I've ever seen faces light up so quickly as when those four saw what we had. I hadn't even known they drank the stuff.

"Here's to the Jebbies (Jesuits); may our lives be happy ones!" And down the hatch it went. I heard later they had hangovers the next morning. Barb and I didn't get the assistance of liquor the day we left for the Convent. Girls were not supposed to drink.

POSTULANT YEAR

I can still see Dad and me as we stood on the sidewalk outside our home the day I entered the convent. It was a beautiful September Sunday afternoon. I had changed from a pretty silk dress to my black postulant outfit and was feeling stilted. Dad put his hands on my shoulders, looked me in the eyes, and said, "Anne, always keep that lovely smile of yours. And if you are ever unhappy come home. We're very proud of you, but we don't want you to be unhappy." I was near tears. "I will, Daddy." I didn't know how hard it would be to keep that promise and how confused I would become regarding the many messages I received about what I should do with my life.

On the way to the convent, Mom, Dad, and I stopped at Barb's house for a last picture-taking session. We knew we would not be allowed to have our pictures taken for the next three years while we were in the Novitiate. It seemed an odd rule to us but we shrugged, realizing it was just another rule we wouldn't understand. Every time I glanced at Barb, she looked like I felt: shell-shocked. Our parents were dressed in their Sunday best and seemed almost desperate to keep the conversation light.

The convent was not the old traditional-looking building on a tree-lined road but a new four-story structure on what was then the edge of town. In addition to being the training grounds for the Sisters of Mercy, it housed the faculty and classrooms for the College of St. Mary.

We all said our tearful good-byes in the convent parlors. Mother Stanislaus, the Sister who would be in charge of us, firmly guided us from our parents to the fourth floor where the postulants and novices lived. We would be spending one year as postulants and two years as novices before leaving the Novitiate. Our timid black-clothed figures followed her sturdy figure down the corridor, hearing for the first time the sound of her rattling rosary beads that would warn us of her approach for the next three years. Finally, Barb and I saw for ourselves what the inside of a convent looked like. We grimaced at each other. We were not thrilled. It was bare and boring.

As we joined the other new recruits in a large room at the end of a very long corridor, I glanced out a window. All I could see were the yet undeveloped fields and little-used roads. I felt in the middle of nowhere. Mother Stanislaus informed us of our activities for the rest of the day. "First you will receive your veil, cuffs, and collars; after that you will have dinner, an hour of recreation with the novices, and then evening prayers followed by night silence." Night Silence? *All night?* Our introduction to the arcane language of convent life began. We were to keep custody of the eyes (avoid eye contact) and not talk with anyone from the time of night prayers until after breakfast the next morning. "You are to clear your minds and think only of God." She didn't smile. She didn't say, "Welcome." We were all very quiet. I was feeling lonesome already and kept praying, "Dear God, please help me." I wanted to talk to Barb, but we were hustled along on our tight schedule with no time for chatter.

The next day felt like a week. The rest of the community was up at 5:00, but we were given the luxury of sleeping until 5:30 and then lined up in the hall outside chapel at 6:00. Our place in line, at meals, and in chapel was according to age so, since Barb and I had the same Birthday, we wound up next to each other. We walked into the big, beautiful chapel single-file, genuflected, and took our places, feeling watched by the other Sisters. After Mass we filed out while the Sisters chanted the morning Office, Latin psalms from the Bible. Finally, we had breakfast at 7:30. Oh, glorious cup of coffee, even if it was in silence. I began appreciating the small things in life.

Later that morning we took college placement tests and registered at the College of Saint Mary. We were assigned classes in Theology, English, Geography, Introduction to Education, Physical Education, and Liturgical Latin. We were not allowed to talk to the college girls and couldn't even speak to the older Sisters, only to the novices and other postulants. For world-class gabbers, this was hard.

The endless morning went into afternoon with more instructions about how to be a good postulant. My first assigned duty, euphemistically called a charge, was washing pots and pans after the supper meal. The pots and pans were huge, the likes of which I had never seen before. Wiping them was awkward and struck me funny. As I stood there laughing, Mother Stanislaus appeared with her frozen frown. "Don't you know this is a silence time, Sister Anne Marie? "Yes, Mother." She had her work cut out for her. She was responsible for about one hundred postulants and novices, most of us in our late teens and early twenties. She felt compelled to show us how to do everything, even wipe a table. "Make sure your rag is damp enough; now here, let me show you!" She kept reminding us to do everything perfectly "all for the honor and glory of God." I kept hoping her approach would soften a bit. It never did.

We had bells for everything. My body did not like getting up at 5:00. But rolling over for a couple more winks was a no-no. We were instructed to "leap out of bed as if it were on fire." This was Nebraska, mind you, and the linoleum floors were cold. A novice was assigned to walk the halls, ringing a cowbell, knocking on each door and saying, "Lord Jesus, preserve us in peace." Barb said later she thought they were saying "Lord Jesus, preserve us in *peaches*." To show we were awake, we were to respond with a loud and clear, "Amen," but mumbles and groans were the common responses. I made heroic efforts to leap but barely rolled out of my nice, warm, comfy bed most mornings.

Our rooms were called cells, of all things, with anywhere from two to eight people in each one. We had a cubicle which we pulled curtains around while dressing and sleeping. It reminded me of a hospital ward. We were relieved to find our beds had sheets (no straw!), a blanket, a pillow, and a white spread. No teddy bears, no radio, just one religious picture was allowed on the nightstand. At the foot of the bed was a hard-backed chair used primarily for draping clothes at night so they would be ready for fast dressing in the morning. We would race to see who could be quickest to the chapel. I never won. I was lucky to arrive in the nick of time for the prayer before meditation. We had been instructed to strip our beds before coming to chapel each morning, so after breakfast we would hurry upstairs to make them before rushing on to the next event.

⌐

When we were allowed to talk, we would spend a great deal of energy discussing the coming August. If we were accepted, we would receive the religious habit of the Sisters of Mercy and be novices for two years. We would also receive new names symbolizing our change of identity and new life dedicated to God. In the meantime, we were called by our secular names. I was officially Sister Anne Marie and had acquired the nickname of SAM, but not in front of Mother Stanislaus. She did not approve of nicknames. She would not have approved of us calling her Mother Stan, either, so we said that in whispers.

During our minimal free time, Barb and I plotted ways to break the boredom. Since there were no mirrors anywhere in the convent, weeks went by without us seeing our reflections. One Saturday we snuck over to the college side of the building to an empty student lounge with a few mirrors. We were shocked at how pitiful our faces looked with pimples and chapped lips; the black dress and veil didn't help us feel cute either. As we grumbled on our way back to the convent, we decided it was a good thing there were no mirrors in the novitiate.

While we were in the student lounge, we had grabbed some cigarette butts from the ashtrays and put them in the bed of one of the novices as a prank. (Cigarettes were a big no-no for us, but the college girls were allowed to smoke.) In the process, I dropped one of the cigarette butts in the hall and went crawling around on my hands and knees looking for it. Luckily, Barb found it on the stairway before Mother Stan could come across it and demand to know how it got there.

To prepare us for the vow of poverty, we were not to use the possessive pronouns "my" or "mine." Everything was the property of the community: our dress, our veil, our books, our dishes, our, our, our. There was no such thing as possession of anything. We were only using the items. It was a difficult thing to remember, especially when discussing MY hands and MY teeth!

The meals also took some adapting. The tables in the refectory (dining room) were in a U-shape and had drawers for dishes. The novices and postulants sat on wooden stools that were tucked under the tables when not in use. Mother Stanislaus made us practice picking up the stools and setting them down very quietly, over and over, until there was almost no sound coming from one hundred stools hitting linoleum. We postulants were at the two ends of the tables, farthest away from Mother Stan, who sat at the head. She wasn't far enough away, though; she was able to notice everything we did. During *silence meals* a novice would read aloud from a spiritual book. Eating in silence and keeping custody of the eyes wore thin so some of us developed a secret signal: we would each take a sip of water and simultaneously slam the glasses down while letting out an "aaaaaah!" Mother didn't like that one. After meals were finished, a couple of novices would bring pans of hot soapy water from the pantry so we could wash our dishes with the person sitting next to us and put them (the dishes, not the person) back in the drawers in front of us. If it was one of the times Mother Stan was mad at us, she would make us stand in silence for what seemed like forever.

At 7:30 P.M. we had an hour of recreation during which we frequently went to the gym for volleyball. How we played in all those clothes still amazes me. We were allowed to change from our black oxfords into white tennis shoes and the postulants could remove the veils, plastic cuffs and collars and pin up the skirts which revealed our lovely black slips. The novices could take off their guimpes (a white starched cloth that covered the chest) and pin back their veils and skirts. Barb and I were usually the last ones chosen for the teams since neither of us was the coordinated, athletic type. It didn't help that we put our arms in front of our faces whenever the ball came near or that we wandered off talking and letting other people hustle for the ball. At least we provided comic relief.

Recreation was followed by The Great Silence which lasted until after breakfast next morning. Standing in line to take a shower was a hard time for me to keep silent. I wanted to ask a question, make a face, *anything*. Even during the day there were long periods of silence, and if we passed a Sister in the hall, the older one was to say, "Let us bless the Lord," and the younger was to respond to her greeting with "Thanks be to God." The first time someone said that to Barb, she couldn't remember the response so blurted, "Awriiiiiiiite!"

Teenager that I was, I would be wide-awake for lights out at 9:30 but in a semi-coma in the morning. Sitting in chapel for meditation and Mass were the sleepiest times. I asked the postulant in the stall (individual seating) behind me to keep an eye on me. When I got precariously close to falling into the aisle, she would lean over and push me upright. I could also fall asleep while standing in line for Holy Communion so the person behind me would have to poke me to get me moving.

The twenty minutes of spiritual reading in chapel before the evening meal was another slump time, and I would often nod off and drop my book. One afternoon some of the college girls were playing a radio so loudly we could hear it in chapel. I was suddenly alert. There was no way I would doze off while "Honeycomb," "That'll be the Day," or "Diana" were blasting away. Several shoulders started shaking with repressed laughter. Mother Stanislaus left the chapel and the music stopped abruptly. The shoulder shaking didn't stop until Mother Stan returned and cleared her throat, a sure sign she was upset with us. Another way she would get our attention was to tap her ring against a pew. We thought it was too bad she couldn't ask God for a thunderclap.

Mother Stanislaus had been the Mistress of Novices and postulants for more years than anybody knew. She was German, and we half-expected her to come out with "You *vill* like it here! You *vill* be proper young Sisters." She acknowledged she was getting too old for the job. "Mother Provincial needs to appoint another Sister who can better understand you young people." We secretly agreed with her. I'm sure it was not easy trying to turn immature girls into mature Sisters. She certainly did give it her best effort, though.

Mother Stan's office was at the corner where two long hallways met. We would avoid that corner by cutting through the B.B.B. (big blue bathroom), especially when she was passing out aspirin. She had a lot of theories about staying healthy: wearing a girdle would prevent a backache, sitting on cold cement would cause kidney problems, aspirin would cure everything, and, if all else failed, take Quinine pills. We would look at her quizzically when she expounded on her theories, but we did what she told us to do, at least while she was looking.

Periodically Mother Stanislaus would weigh each member of our band (what they called the group that entered together). In our first few months, I gained fifteen pounds, and Barb gained fourteen. We didn't much care and blamed most of our weight gain on the yards of black we wore. We didn't know if Mother Stan was worried our band was gaining too much or too little. Eating was one pleasurable thing she didn't tell us to quit doing. The only stipulation about food was we had to take a little of everything and clean our plates. The meals were traditional mid-western fare: meat, potatoes, vegetables, bread, milk, and dessert. Institutional cooking made the food bland but most of us were usually so hungry we ate with gusto.

Friday evenings during the football season were difficult

for those of us who had spent the last few years going to Prep's football games. Since we didn't have access to a radio, a TV, or even a newspaper, we had no idea how Prep was doing. We tormented ourselves by sneaking over to a classroom on the college side and watching the college girls leave the dorm with Friday night dates, fantasizing what we might be doing if we weren't in a convent. Who knew if any of them were going to a football game. We just assumed they were. On Saturday mornings, the priest who said Mass genuflected near the youngest postulant and, in a stage whisper, would say the football score of the night before. We loved him for that.

The weekend schedules were relatively relaxed. We could sleep until 6:00. There were no classes, but we were kept busy anyway. "Idle hands make the devil's workshop." I was assigned to work in the garden picking tomatoes, cantaloupes, green peppers, parsley, and watermelon. It was news to me how to do it. I'd never been near a vegetable garden, let alone do something productive in one.

One Saturday, Barb and I decided we'd had enough of this organized labor so, while the rest of the postulants were busy sewing on name tags or doing something equally boring, we hot-footed it up The Hill. It was a lovely, isolated, wooded place with an old building which housed the Provincial Council, the governing body for the Western Province. We would sit under a walnut tree and laugh about nothing. One Saturday we got caught. Along came THE BRASS: Mother Provincial, the Assistant Mother Provincial, and the Mother Superior. We didn't know whether to start running or sit there and face the music. We faced the music. But they just talked about the weather and the beautiful grounds, told us not to eat too many walnuts, and walked on! We sat there stunned.

That was one of the few times we did not get reprimanded. We thought we were in for it, though. As soon as we got back to the novitiate, Mother Stan called for Barb. We were sure one of The Brass had snitched on us. But, no, Barb's parents were on the phone. Later, we decided Mother was having a rare moment of weakness by allowing Barb a brief chat. We were not allowed phone calls except when Mother deemed it necessary, usually for something serious like an illness or death in the family. One time, Mother actually asked a postulant if she knew how to use the phone.

Barb came out of Mother Stan's office excited about having talked to her parents but very lonesome. We walked up the (permitted) back road to talk and cry. Barb turned in the direction of her home and shouted, "Maaaaaa!" It made her feel better. We spent many hours walking up and down that gravel road the next few years, talking about how lonesome we were and how we didn't know if we could do this convent thing. One of our teachers told us that during her first year, she and other postulants would say to each other, "Let's stay and see what we're having for dinner." It was their way of persevering one meal at a time. I didn't find much consolation in that approach. It's hard to say, looking back, how long I would have stayed if I hadn't had Barb. We propped each other up and dragged each other down, whatever was the mood of the moment.

Mother Stan told the postulants over and over that if God didn't want us to be Sisters of Mercy, she and the Provincial Council would advise us to leave. Until that happened, it was simply the devil tempting us when we questioned being there. She also said if we walked away from a religious vocation, our lives would not work; we would probably marry alcoholics, have crippled children, get cancer, be disowned by our families, and on and on. Once we left we could not come back. I certainly did not want my life to be ruined because I was not doing God's will! I felt trapped, as if there were something missing in that logic but I couldn't figure out what. As usual, Barb and I coped by making a joke, "God, get down here and talk to me now! If I'm going to be a bride of Christ, I need better communication!"

∽

Visiting Sundays were very stressful. We were allowed to see family once a month the first year and then, as novices, only three times a year for the next two years. Seeing our families just reminded us how much we missed them. We would spend the Saturday evening before visits ironing our postulant dresses, shining our shoes, and trying to calm the flutters in our stomachs. After Sunday breakfast, as we took our week's worth of dirty clothes to the laundry, we usually talked about things we were going to tell our parents. "Do you think my parents would understand if we told them about night silence or silence during meals?" "Uh, maybe not."

Mother Stanislaus would assign each of us a parlor to use while we visited. My heart ached when I saw Mom and Dad. I couldn't tell them how things really were, so I spent a lot of energy playing the role of happy postulant, just like they spent the time playing the role of happy family. Marty, who was almost ten years old, would get bored and wander off to see if she could get into the convent part of the building. She didn't get to see much before being escorted back to us. I certainly understood her curiosity. Sometimes Paul and Bruce came and were equally bored. Sitting around a convent parlor wasn't exactly their idea of a fun time. Every once in a while Mom would tell me about seeing Patrick's mother who would approach Mom and Dad after Sunday church with, "I simply must tell you about Patrick!" and bend her ear with details about his life in the seminary. I don't remember being terribly interested at that point, but I thought it was funny that his mother was still as obsessed with Patrick as she was during grade school when she was a hovering room mother.

Mother Stanislaus would visit with each family at some point in the afternoon. She got along with Mom and Dad until she said she was now my mother. I knew Mother Stanislaus considered us her spiritual children, but telling Mom and Dad sounded harsh. I was pretty good at reading their faces by that time in my life and I knew they had been hurt. It was hard enough giving up a daughter to a convent without a stranger acting as if she could replace them. We continued to chat as if nothing had happened and at 4:40 on the button, the bell for spiritual reading rang. We were expected to leave for chapel immediately. No lingering good-byes.

Very few of us concentrated on our spiritual reading after an afternoon visiting with family. A feeling of panic would come over me, and I would wonder what I was doing. We had been told we must "surmount nature and not identify ourselves with family interests." We were not to let our visits distract us in any way or cause us to think worldly thoughts. I couldn't fathom how family could be bad for me and I couldn't help but question if letting go of them would ever get any easier. Praying didn't cut it for me; I never felt transformed by the power of prayer. In fact, I usually felt more empty, as if I were doing it wrong, and praying about it didn't help one whit. I kept trying, though.

The novices were aware of our sadness so did what they could to help us through the evening. They understood what we were experiencing and said that things would get easier for us, as it evidently had for them. They planned a party with the theme of Alice in Wonderland, a quite appropriate theme since I felt I had fallen in a rabbit hole. As we left the chapel for supper, a novice stood at the refectory door dressed as the Mad Hatter with a white nightgown over her habit and huge rabbit ears over her veil. She had us take paper teapots from a battered old black hat and sit at a table with the matching teapot. Not only did we get to sit at a different table with different people, we were allowed to talk through dinner! Later, during recreation, the novices gave a program about the difficult days of being a postulant. One of the skits was about us:

Praying in stalls but we're not horses
Doing charges but we're not soldiers
Being in a band but we're not musicians
Living in cells but we're not prisoners.
The evening was fun, but I still cried myself to sleep.

⤙

There were several times it was obvious we needed cheering up. On a lovely fall afternoon, Mother Stan had an older Sister pack some candy and take us on an outing to a new Catholic cemetery with lots of open grassy areas just across the highway. It was our first time off the property since entering, and we were determined to have fun even if it was in a cemetery. Five of us wandered away from the group and then got a lecture for running to catch up. "You can't act like young girls any more; you have to realize you are becoming Sisters of Mercy and must act like ladies in public," the older Sister chided. Good thing she hadn't seen us right before that. We had pulled down our thick black hose to get some sun and were laughing at our hairy legs. When we realized everyone else had moved on, we pulled our hose up and jumped over the bushes. We didn't *try* to do the wrong thing; it just came naturally. A few of the other postulants were very serious and would not even think of doing something silly. We were serious, too, but got tired of following the rules ALL-THE-TIME!

We had daily schedules that left very little time for goofing-off. In addition to charges, prayers, classes, and studies we had an hour a week in the sewing room to make the habits we would receive in August. The habit was originally a simple dress of the Victorian Era and meant to be unobtrusive. It was anything *but* unobtrusive in 1957 with its yards of black serge and starched white. We were expected to sew everything, including the veils, dominos (a cloth covering worn under the veils), coifs, and guimpes (white starched parts around the face and chest). They had to be done *perfectly*; if an edge was even 1/8 of an inch off, it had to be ripped out and re-done. The strangest item to make was the night coif. After receiving the habit, we were to have something on our heads at all times, even at night. We figured the reason was because our hair would be short and our heads might get cold. Our hair would be short all right.

We also spent three hours a week in the hot, stuffy laundry room which was in a separate building. To entertain ourselves we had contests to see which two postulants could fold sheets the fastest—in silence, of course. Sometimes we would have to iron veils and dominos on the mangle (a machine for ironing laundry by pressing it between heated surfaces). We called it mangling veils and playing dominos. Afterward we raced to class feeling very hot and very wrinkled.

The postulants had regular lecture sessions with Mother Stan, during which she made valiant attempts to instruct us on the fine art of being a Religious Sister of Mercy. For example, she thought we needed to understand the difference between a *Nun* and a *Sister*: "A Nun is completely cloistered with little or no contact with the outside world and takes the vow of silence along with her vows of poverty, chastity, and obedience. Sisters, on the other hand, have contact with the outside world because they teach and nurse; they don't take the vow of silence. You are in training to be Sisters, not Nuns." Good thing. It was hard enough for us to keep silent part of the day without taking a vow to never speak. Mother Stan added that nurses in England are also called Sisters. No wonder people didn't know what to call us. We continued to use the terms interchangeably.

Saturdays amazed me. There was always something different to keep us busy. After breakfast one Saturday, Barb and I were assigned to pluck chickens. I didn't think anything about it until we headed for the basement, got a whiff of the dead chickens, and saw the blood. Barb mumbled something about needing another apron and vanished. She up and left! Obedient me, I stayed and cleaned and gagged. It was a while before I could enjoy eating chicken again.

Later that morning I found Barb drying her hair and looking as if nothing had happened. "I just couldn't handle dead chickens this morning, Annie." She was having a lousy day that started with not hearing the rising bell. I wondered how the sam-hill someone could not hear that bell. She had raced to get dressed, and just as she got to the chapel for Meditation discovered she had forgotten her handkerchief, which she couldn't live without. Since we were not allowed to use the one elevator in the building, she ran up the four flights of stairs (eighty-eight steps; we had counted) and back down trying to look composed as she walked into chapel.

The reason Barb was washing her hair in the middle of the morning was because Mother Stan would not let us wash our hair in the shower at night. She thought we might catch colds if we went to bed with wet heads and then we would need more aspirin. When weather permitted we dried our hair outside. Since there were very few warm, sunny Saturday mornings in Omaha, Barb was in the utility room with the space heater, which was our other option. As I talked with her the heater blew a fuse and all the lights went out. Mother Stan was there in a flash, fixed the fuse, and left the room. The fuse blew again. Mother came back looking like she was ready to blow a fuse herself.

We decided we'd better get out of everyone's hair, if they had hair to get out of, and went back up to the forbidden hill. While climbing a tree, I broke my plastic collar and cuffs. Most of us avoided asking Mother Stan for new ones because we would invariably get a lecture on being careful. We kept stapling the old ones even though the staples pinched the fine hairs on our necks and arms. We would have contests to see who could have the most staples in her collar and cuffs before Mother Stan noticed and made us ask for new ones.

We ended that long Saturday with one last frustration. We were hungry and had asked Mother if we could have some apples. Just as we started eating them, the bell rang for night prayers. We were not allowed to save food or throw it away. So there we were outside chapel cramming apples in our mouths, laughing and chewing all the way up the aisle to our stalls. Mother had to clear her throat twice before we could control ourselves. I was glad for night and silence so I could just crawl into bed. I was so tired of being reprimanded.

Once a month on a Sunday we could write letters to our families. Mother Stan read the letters. If she didn't like what we had written she made us re-do them. We were limited to two pages apiece so Barb would use tiny, tiny handwriting telling her parents every little detail. I wrote normally. I didn't think Mom and Dad would enjoy reading my letters with a magnifying glass. Mother Stan also screened incoming mail, which she handed out to us on Saturday evenings. We figured she was looking for love letters from old boyfriends or even the mention of old boyfriends.

On those letter writing Sundays, we would sit around in the common room comparing what we were writing. Since it was one of the few times we were not closely supervised, we would frequently get sidetracked gabbing. One topic always came up: Reception of the Habit in August at which time we would be given a new name as part of changing our identity. We were allowed to give three choices to the Provincial Council but couldn't pick one already taken by any of the other hundreds of Sisters of Mercy. We frantically worked at finding decent names so the Council would not assign us something we wouldn't want to spend the rest of our lives being called, like Sister Mary Bartholomew or Sister Mary Mergatroid. The names had to include a form of Mary (Marie, Marian, etc.) in honor of the Blessed Virgin Mary. We wondered why men were not expected to change their names when they became priests. At the time, we had very little awareness of how chauvinistic the Catholic Church was, and how very differently women were treated from men.

～

We knew we were in trouble one Sunday evening when Mother Stan called the postulants together for a special lecture. She was in a serious mood. Her frown was deeper than usual. First, she informed us we could not shave our legs any more. I figured she was just over-reacting to Barb's having cut her legs with a razor the night before.

Barb had already told me the story: "I borrowed your razor, Annie, because I didn't have any sharp blades left in my razor, oops, *our* razor. I should have gotten a lawn mower, but it was too late. Anyway, like a dummy, I loosened the blade and zapped up and down in a hurry. As I was putting the razor away, I looked down and was standing in a pool of blood! I panicked. I poured Cashmere Bouquet powder all over my legs to stop the bleeding. It didn't help. I dashed to my cell and, without thinking, threw the bloody towel on the bedspread. It left a huge spot so I grabbed it and dropped it... on a white t-shirt! Finally, I tied my legs in handkerchiefs and slept between two blankets so I wouldn't get more blood on the sheets. Don't ask me why. I didn't think I could break night silence by telling anyone. Of course I had to tell Mother about it in the morning so I could get clean sheets, towels, and blankets. She didn't think it was funny."

The other, larger bomb Mother dropped during that lecture was the Chapter of Faults. Once a month, she intoned, we would be expected to kneel beside our chair during lecture and state our infractions against the rules. You could hear the old pin drop in the room. Nobody was breathing. We knew we weren't going to like this one. Going to a priest for confession once a week was enough without stating things we did wrong in front of the whole group. Mother said it was to help us to become more humble. We quickly figured out our biggest challenge would be mentioning an infraction that did not implicate others. For example, a couple of nights before, a few of us postulants and novices had gone down to a tunnel that connected to the college. The novices had hidden a gallon of fermented grape juice and two loaves of fresh cinnamon bread. Of course we were not supposed to be down there, let alone eating, drinking, laughing, and trying to get looped on grape juice during a time of silence. That was not the kind of thing that could be mentioned in Chapter of Faults.

⌒

By November we had caught on to how things worked in a convent, appreciating the rare official times we could talk, laugh, and have fun. We looked forward to Feast Days because they were first-class days, which meant talking at all three meals. On second-class days, we could talk at lunch and dinner; on third-class days we talked only at dinner. On silence days, there was no talking until recreation in the evening. By then we were usually fit to be tied.

Mother Stans' Feast Day, the day the church honors St. Stanislaus, was a first-class day for us in the novitiate. Barb and I took on the job of directing a program in honor of the day. We knew we could come up with something funny and creative. For two weeks before, we were in a frenzy of writing, convincing others they wanted to participate, and rehearsing. Mother Provincial invited herself and the Council to see the play, which gave us the last minute jitters. It went off beautifully with a few exceptions, like Barb's having nothing to sit on as she walked onstage to play the piano. The Council and Mother Stanislaus loved the program and laughed at all the right places. They even brought us Cokes to drink. We never got Cokes. Barb, who lived on Cokes before entering, illegally saved half of hers to sip on later.

November brought the usual Nebraska snowstorms, canceling all the schools until the snowplows could be dug out. As soon as the blowing and snowing stopped, several of us ventured out to build a snowman. Getting ready to go outside was as much work as bundling up when we were kids. Mother Stan insisted we wear galoshes, a shawl pinned snugly under the chin, sweater, and gloves. In no time at all, we were sopping wet, in spite of our bundling. My stockings came unrolled and were hanging down over my ankles making us laugh so hard we fell in a snow-bank. (Many of us had given up wearing garter belts and rolled our stockings at the knees, a much faster process but harder on the circulation.) We didn't want our snowman to melt, so we put it in the walk-in freezer near the kitchen. It didn't last long there, either. We were told to get the thing out of there *immediately*.

Hanging around Barb was not always fun, especially when she was crying about wanting to go home, but at least there was never a dull moment. One afternoon she was telling me about her day when we both realized we had one minute to get to class in the adjoining building. We dashed into the hallway and ran smack into a novice, knocking her books all over the floor. After apologizing and helping put her glasses and books back in place, we raced to class. By then, the only empty chairs were in front. This particular teacher hated latecomers and did not tolerate anything but intense concentration on her every word. "And just what is the matter that the two of you are out of breath and laughing again?" She never did come to like us.

Later that afternoon, six of us had sewing class back in the convent. The elderly Sister who was teaching us sat in one corner of the room at her sewing machine, attempting to enforce perfect sewing and silence. Barb was feeling good about doing a nice job on a white guimpe until she turned it over to find she had sewn a chunk of black wool to the other side. She looked at me and whispered, "Ah, we rip what we sew." For once, I controlled myself. Then, when her sewing machine ran out of thread, Barb walked over to get a spool, returned to her machine, and found her thread was still attached to the other side of the room. I snorted. The other four postulants kept busy at their sewing machines trying, without success, not to snicker. We all had to sit in silence with our hands folded for ten minutes after that.

The coif was the hardest part to sew because it had to fit perfectly around the face and head so no hair could be seen. About that time, we got the official word that, yes, all those rumors were true and we would have our hair shaved off the day after we received the habit. After the initial shave we could wear it any length we wanted as long as it didn't show. Things were getting more serious by the day, and we wondered what was coming next. Whenever we were faced with something we didn't like, Mother Stan would advise us to thank God anyway. "He gives you blessings that you don't know are blessings." When Mother Stan was not around, we would very piously say, "Thank You God," and then mumble, "Dang It."

⌒

Christmas came and went quickly. The holidays were a tad bit different in the convent. No fun parties. No shopping in decorated department stores with snow falling outside and Christmas music in the background. We tried to make the novitiate look festive by decorating with holly and drawing scenes on the windows in the recreation room. We spent hours crocheting around the edges of holy pictures which we would give as presents to our families.

I missed being home at Christmas time but I didn't miss the roller-coaster of emotions that had come with the holidays the last few years. Mom would get weepy Christmas Eve, especially when she thought about Mary Jo. Then she would continue drinking, and the rest of us would feel on edge wondering what she would do next. Her sentences would cease to make sense. I kept hoping each Christmas would be different and we would all go to Midnight Mass after opening presents. But things didn't change. Mom and Dad would go up to bed, Bruce and Paul would meet their friends, and Marty would disappear in our bedroom. I would sit in the living room with the Christmas tree lights, crying and wondering what had happened.

Mom and Dad didn't have a clue what to give a postulant for Christmas, so I received boxes of candy. Mother Stan kept most of the sweets we received and periodically doled them out. Barb's mom gave her homemade terry cloth aprons, but Mother Stan wouldn't let her keep them, saying terry cloth wasn't one of the materials we were allowed to have. News to us. I felt sorry for her mom when Barb had to return the aprons.

Barb's folks became very lonesome during the holidays and would park outside the convent hoping to catch a glimpse of her. Sometimes I was jealous of all the attention she received from them, but I didn't think I could handle my parents coming around as much as hers did. It was too hard on the heart. One afternoon, Barb and I were walking outside and saw her parents' car at the top of the gravel road. But rules were rules, and she couldn't go talk with them. Instead, she waved her white handkerchief. She was concentrating so hard on looking at her Mom and Dad, she walked smack into a big puddle of mud. They sent her dog, Cookie, down the hill with a candy bar and a note attached to the collar. Barb was near tears kneeling on the ground hugging her. It was a good thing Mother Stan was not watching out the fourth floor convent window. Or maybe she was.

⌒

The Feast of Holy Innocence, which honored infant saints, was in the last week of December and meant a celebration for us, because we were the "infants" of the convent. Rules were dropped for a whole twelve hours. It felt like being sprung free. The night before, a novice read us the schedule for the day:

Rising: optional
Talking: anytime, anywhere
Breakfast: at your convenience
Brunch: 12:30…at your own risk
Rest of the day: on your own

I woke up at 9:45 and felt like I had died and gone to heaven. The first thing I did was eat a piece of fudge I had pilfered from Barb's illegal stash. I would have stayed in bed all day, but I didn't want to miss any of the fun. Six of us met in the big blue bathroom and, after much chattering, decided to start with breakfast.

"Shall we meet in the lobby, dahling, and then decide where to go?"

"Ah, yes, such decisions. Will it be the refectory or the refectory?"

"They both have such good cuisine."

The refectory was wonderfully noisy with postulants laughing, milling about, slamming down stools as noisily as they could, and eating heavenly *hot* buttered toast.

For brunch, the novices had us put towels around our necks as bibs, galoshes on our feet as booties, and ribbons in our hair. The youngest postulant sat at the head of the table acting as much like Mother Stan as she dared, clearing her throat and rapping her knuckle on the table for attention. Mother Stan sat at the far end and wore a white novice veil instead of her usual black one and tried to relax enough to laugh at our antics. The meal was served haphazardly: dessert first, then peas in the gravy bowl with a big kitchen fork, potatoes, gravy with a sieve, and fried chicken. Milk was slopped from a big pan with a dipper. Almost everyone joined in the spirit of the day and became quite rowdy. Some pretended to misbehave and were told to sit in the corner. We were excused from saying any of our usual daily prayers. A rosary was the only thing required which was no small thing since it took a good fifteen minutes with all the Hail Marys and Our Fathers. A couple of the postulants couldn't quite handle the lack of rules and said all their prayers anyway. I found that hard to comprehend. It was so much fun to have fun-legally!

∽

Six new postulants joined our band in February. I felt sorry for them, learning all the rules, but not sorry enough to spare the teasing. We old-timers told them a few rules we had made up:

Wear your veils to the bathroom at night

Wear your stockings at all times, even in the shower

Allow no one to see your legs

Put on your nightgown before removing your underclothes

They believed us for a while. The real rules were so confusing and arbitrary, it's no wonder they swallowed anything we told them.

∽

March was vocation month when we said extra prayers for other girls to join us. The thirteen of us who had graduated from Mercy High spent a day at the school to do our part in recruiting. Our pictures were posted on the main bulletin board and we felt like VIPs. Barb played the piano at an assembly for the several hundred students. I was glad I didn't have a particular talent to show off. I would have been paralyzed with nervousness. Several seniors confided they were planning on entering the convent in September. When they asked me what it was like, I didn't know what to say. It's hard to explain in a hundred words or less. Plus, I didn't know how much I could really tell them or should tell them. So I kept it vague. That worked on me when I was a senior.

Barb and I wandered backstage after the program to look at props we had used during our junior and senior years. Such memories came rushing at us! The door and window frame from our spring play was in a closet. The lattices from our junior prom stood in the corner. Barb's dad and her boyfriend had helped make them. A big cardboard candy cane from our Candy Cane Ball was in a box. We looked at the backstage SILENCE sign and toyed with the idea of giving it to Mother Stan but figured she wouldn't think it was very funny. We both felt like crying. "We're history already!" We talked about the last dance we had, the last romance of our high school days, the last pretty dresses we wore. On the way back to the convent all of us were very quiet. The emotion of getting ready and the anticipation of seeing the outside world again reminded us we had been out of circulation a long time. A couple of us had been so excited about being out in public we had almost gotten carsick that morning. Seeing the enthusiasm for the religious life from so many students was almost worth the nausea. The students had caught a sort of convent fever that day, and it helped me feel better about my choice. I was so unsure of being where I was that I was constantly looking for validation. I kept feeling I was *supposed* to be there and the doubts never went away. I kept feeling as if I were all dressed up in the wrong costume, an actor in the wrong play.

⌣

Easter was my favorite time of the year. After the six weeks of Lent, deprivation, and dreary Nebraska winter days, no wonder I loved it. To prepare for Easter, we had more silence days, minimal times of relaxing the rules, and a barren, undecorated chapel. Easter meant flowers and warmer weather, all the things that felt soothing to the soul. It was also a visiting Sunday. We asked permission the evening before to go to the trunk room and resurrect (no pun intended) some new black hose out of the deep corners of our trunks. Mother Stan had made us darn our old ones until the darns needed darning and were leaving blisters on our heels.

Mom and Dad put on a brave face as they came into the parlor but I could tell they were worried about Mary Jo. She had caught pneumonia and was not recovering very quickly. Her constant seizures had weakened her and made her vulnerable to infections. From what Mom and Dad said, Beatrice State Home was taking good care of her but I sensed they wished someone could do more. Once again, they had to watch helplessly as a daughter came close to death. We didn't talk much about her, which was our usual way of dealing with difficult situations. I realized that Sunday how much I missed Mary Jo's laugh and her simple, loving companionship. I would get a fleeting memory of her and then shut down so I wouldn't cry.

Mother Stanislaus left us alone for our visit that afternoon. I think she knew Mary Jo was very ill. She focused on other groups instead and discovered several young men visiting a postulant. Since she had not met these males before, she assumed they were old boyfriends and told them to go home. It turned out three of them were the postulant's brothers, and one was her parish priest out of uniform. They stayed. Mother did have to send one of Barb's old boyfriends home, though.

That evening we played volleyball again to let off steam. Actually, some of us sat and talked while others played. I didn't say anything about Mary Jo; again, I didn't know how. Another postulant entertained us with stories about her goofy boyfriends; she once gave a guy thirty dollars to buy an engagement ring... for another girl. I laughed myself silly. Then someone in the group remembered my infamous thinking-of-the-blessed-Virgin-Mary-on-a-date incident and I got more razzing.

During night silence Barb handed me a toy she had confiscated from the things my family brought for Easter. It was a cute little animal that beat a very loud drum. I took it from her not realizing she had wound it up. Good grief, now what? Gripping it tightly, I waited until Barb went to take a shower. Then I stuffed the thing under her pillow so it would drum away when she got into bed.

College classes became overwhelming. Mother Stan lectured us about setting an example as Sisters and getting good grades. I was never much of a curve-raiser and wasn't sure I wanted to be or could be. That spring, just trying to complete term papers became a challenge. Those of us who functioned best under pressure had planned on typing the final drafts of our papers the Sunday before they were due. It should have been a breeze. We trotted over to the college typing room first thing after breakfast. The rooms were locked! Nobody types on Sunday? Locating the key took thirty minutes, typing the first two pages took two hours. Well, not to worry, we had all afternoon. Wrong. Mother Stan announced at lunch we would have a special lecture, followed by choir practice. We panicked. No way she would excuse us from either function. I was frustrated and angry, but there was nothing I could do about it. I couldn't even verbalize that I was frustrated and angry. Expressing anger was not allowed. We were supposed to consider anything Mother told us to do as God's will and things would work out if we were obedient.

So I went to the lecture given by two hermits from Italy. (We thought that sounded like the name of a play. Or a restaurant.) They talked about coming to America to found a new monastery and brought with them a tall, dark, and definitely handsome priest from California to interpret. Well, all of a sudden, I wasn't so sorry I had to be there. I hadn't looked at anything that interesting in a long, long time. Term paper? What term paper?

Reality hit again after supper, so we asked Mother if we could finish typing instead of going to recreation. No. Like good little Sisters we recreated and went to bed wondering how we were going to manage. First thing in the morning after breakfast, we hot-footed it to the typing room and finished just in the nick of time. Learning spirituality was stressful.

After final exams, we had to help with cleaning in the convent and dorms while the students were on Spring break. We scrubbed windows, washed screens, mopped floors, and dusted bookshelves. We couldn't miss a speck of dirt, or Mother Stan made us do it over. When we were cleaning the Council Room, Mother Provincial had pity on us and played some music. We wished they had a romantic Johnny Mathis album but gladly listened to Mantovani instead. Hearing *any* music was a novelty for us.

⤴

The postulants took turns serving meals. It was one of those things assigned by age which meant Barb and I wound up together again. The chocolate milk was running low during dinner one evening so we both rushed to the walk-in refrigerator for more. Barb grabbed a can only to discover it was sour. In her haste to keep looking, she splashed it all over us and on the shelves of food. I grabbed a rag to wipe off the pans of Jell-O and whispered, "I feel like I'm patting a baby's tummy!" which cracked us both up just as Mother Stan appeared in the doorway clearing her throat. I often wondered if she ever thought we were funny.

One hundred and eleven days before receiving the habit (who was counting?), we sneaked a coif, guimpe, domino and veil from a novice's room, hid in a bathroom tub room, and took turns trying them on. Of course there were no mirrors so we had to tell each other how we looked. It all felt so cumbersome. Our hands and face were the only skin that showed. No wonder children looked at Sisters and asked, "Do you have ears?" "Are you a boy or a girl?" "What color is your hair?" We didn't leave the habit on for long; we were afraid Mother Stan would find us. She was so good at that sort of thing.

⤴

Spring was a very difficult time for me. We were allowed very few movies but during that time we saw *Song of Bernadette.* I watched it with a heavy heart. During the scene in which Bernadette leaves for the convent, I cried, remembering my feelings the day I entered. In another scene, the Blessed Virgin Mary tells Bernadette she would not be happy on earth, only in heaven. What a scary thought! When Bernadette developed a cancerous tumor on her knee, she would not let the other sisters take her to Lourdes to be cured. It was all so overwhelming for me. I didn't want to suffer all my life. I wanted to enjoy my life as much as I could. I prayed for understanding, but, again, I was left to figure it out on my own.

About that same time, a couple of postulants decided they did not want to stay. The hardest part of their leaving was the silence surrounding it. Nothing was said or discussed. The first we knew about it was in chapel when we noticed their empty stalls. By the next time we were in chapel the seating arrangement had been redone. Not only did I miss the ones who left but I was envious someone else had been able to make a decision that I wondered if I was supposed to make. Barb and I would talk about how real our vocations were, or were not, but our conversations only went in circles, resolving nothing.

In May my sister Mary Jo died. It was her birthday month. She had just turned twenty, the age the pediatrician predicted she would die. I knew she was dead before Mom and Dad came to the convent to tell me. I'd had a dream the night before, during which she kept waving good-bye. I went to the funeral home and the burial at the cemetery, accompanied by an older Sister of Mercy. I was not allowed to go home. I felt so sad for Mom and Dad. They needed me to go home with them. They had always thought of Mary Jo and me together, and I would have been a great comfort to them. But, no. Rules were Rules. When I came back to the convent, nobody said anything to me about her and I didn't know what to say. Again, I kept my feelings inside. I wanted to cry but couldn't. I didn't know how to grieve. It was many years before I was finally able to let myself feel the terrible loss of Mary Jo's death. I think my life would have been very different had she been a normal older sister. I would have had someone with whom to talk and to share what was going on. Chances are, we would have been very close.

Ceremonial reception of the habit.

August 16, 1958

Ceremonial reception of the habit

The postulants, religious, and clergy are followed by the celebrant as they proceed into the chapel.

The choir sings "O Glorious Virgin."

The celebrant blesses the candles and presents them to the postulants. The lighted candle symbolizes the divine wisdom and illuminating fervor of the holy spirit.

The celebrant interrogates the postulants as to their freedom to receive the habit and their motives for doing it.

The postulants leave the chapel. The celebrant blesses the habits, cinctures and church cloaks, which have been placed with the veils, rosaries, and crucifixes at the epistle side of the altar.

A little later, the postulants return, clothed as novices in the religious habit. The choir sings: who is she that cometh up from the desert, flowing with delights, leaning upon her beloved? Thou art fair my beloved, meek and beautiful. Come, o my spouse, from libanus, come from libanus; come, thou shalt be crowned.

The celebrant turns to the new novices, makes the sign of the cross over them, and says the investiture prayers.

The new novices standing say: the empire of the world and the grandeur of this earth, I have despised for the love of our lord Jesus Christ, whom I have seen, whom I have loved, and in whom I have believed, and towards whom my heart inclineth.

The novices prostrate, signifying their total dedication to god. During this time the "veni creator" (come holy spirit) is sung followed by the prayers of the celebrant. He then sprinkles holy water, after which the novices rise and return to their places.

NOVICE YEARS

We were giddy with excitement the day we received the habit. We were wearing the religious habit of the Sisters of Mercy! My teenage idealism had taken over, and I was swept up in the fervor of serving God and saving the world. I was two days short of nineteen, an age known for its idealism and black-and-white thinking. I wanted to do something outstanding with my life and was convinced this was it. During the ceremony, I was so excited my hands were shaking and the veins in my neck were throbbing.

Our biggest challenge during the ceremony was changing from the postulant outfit to the habit while the visitors waited in the chapel. We were instructed, of course, to do so in complete silence and with custody of the eyes. We had practiced the ceremony over and over the week before until we knew it by heart. At recreation the night before, a postulant had commented, "In one part of the ceremony it says something about coming from Libanus. Where is Libanus?" Barb didn't miss a beat and said, "It's in New Jersey, you jerk!" We laughed until we cried. I thought of Barb's comment the next day as I caught a glimpse of her solemn face while a novice cropped her hair. (The actual head shaving would come the next day when there was more time.) We were in a big room near the chapel and could hear the organ music and the choir filling in the minutes of waiting. We removed our familiar old postulant dresses and struggled to put on the unfamiliar, bulky habits. Each one of us had a novice helping, but it still seemed to take forever. Finally, after much arranging and shifting, (especially with the white wool church cloaks) we lined up and made our grand entrance from the back of the chapel. I heard gasps and sobs. I snuck a glance but could not locate Mom and Dad. I felt so important receiving all this attention. It was hard to concentrate on the rest of the ceremony. I wanted to fiddle with my habit. It was such a strange sensation to move in all that material, and I couldn't help but wonder how I looked. I felt like a different person.

We proceeded very formally to the front of the chapel where Mother Provincial approached each one to announce our new names. "Sister Anne Marie Fangman, you will now be known as Sister Mary Janice." I would have a decent name! Next, we prostrated on the chapel floor, a feat Mother Stan had made us practice until we did it to perfection. It meant all 30 of us simultaneously kneeling and then lying flat with arms outstretched on the marble floor. Being face down with all that material felt like being wrapped in about three blankets. Our next challenge was getting back up without losing our balance. All those rehearsals worked and no one tripped.

Seeing our families and each other after the ceremony was the next excitement. Mom and Dad chatted with other parents while we grilled each other about our names, how we felt, and how we looked in our new garb. I noticed Mom's face. She was so beautiful but she was showing the stress of losing three of her children in one year: Mary Jo's death, Bruce's leaving for the Army, and my going to the convent. She looked tired, she hardly smiled, and she talked even less than usual. Dad tried to pretend that everything was fine like he usually did.

～

The next day was full of adjustments to the habit. Going up stairs, I would forget to lift up the floor-length skirt and find myself walking up the inside if the hem. I didn't feel very grown-up landing on my hands and knees halfway up the steps. The older novices eventually showed us how to swing each leg around back and on to the next step to get the material out of the way. This trick came in handy when our arms were full of books and we couldn't lift up the front of the habit. It looked a bit spastic, but it worked. The stiff coif left red dents on my jaws and caused pimples to break out where it rubbed. The starched guimpe rubbed my Adam's apple, and when I reached out in front of me, the guimpe popped in my face. Other than that, I was fine.

There was a prescribed ritual in the morning as we dressed: we were to kiss each piece of the habit while thinking of what the item symbolized, silently saying a special prayer which was printed on a card on our nightstand:

HABIT: The black surge dress went over the layer of undergarments: "Clothe my soul with the nuptial robe of charity that I may carry it pure and undefiled before the judgment seat."

CINCTURE: A black leather belt was wrapped around the waist as a reminder to be obedient in all actions. "O Lord Jesus Christ, who became obedient unto death, even to the death of the cross, grant me the true spirit of religious obedience."

ROSARY: The rosary with its black wooden cross and smaller white cross inside the black represented dying to self every day. "O Lord Jesus Christ, grant me the grace to deny myself, to take up my cross daily and follow Thee. Mother of Mercy, pray for me now and at the hour of my death."

GUIMPE: The large white bib was tied around the neck while praying: "Create in me, O Lord, a clean heart and renew a right spirit within me."

COIF: The white starched headdress signified belonging to Christ. "Place Thyself, O Lord, as a seal upon my forehead that I may be of the number."

DOMINO AND VEIL: Finally, the inner and outer head coverings went over the coif: "Place on my head the helmet of salvation and give me power against my enemies. O Mary Immaculate, obtain for me perfect purity of soul and body."

In addition to all of the above, we were to wear voluminous black formal sleeves when we went to chapel, had visitors, or left the premises. When we walked we were to put our hands together under the sleeves. At the top of each sleeve was a cloth loop that hooked to a button on the shoulder of the habit. When not in use, the sleeves hung in the cloakroom along with the white wool cloaks that were worn for special ceremonies in the chapel. Scrambling to the cloakroom, hooking on our sleeves, and rushing up the stairs to chapel was a ritual we were expected to do in silence once the bell for chapel had rung. On the special occasions we added the cloak, we often had to (silently) ask another sister for help with maneuvering it under the veil and over the shoulders.

Barb and I grabbed moments here and there to compare notes about being novices. She liked her new name, too, which was Sister Mary Ellen. In private, though, we still called each other Barbie and Annie. During recreation, she and I tried to make a joke about having no hair. We would mimic combing our long locks by bending to the side, "brushing" to our knees, and flipping the pretend hair over our shoulders. We got quite a few laughs from the other novices but we never performed our routine when Mother Stanislaus was around.

We were called canonicals, or first-year novices. This was the year devoted primarily to our spiritual development as dictated by Canon (Church) Law. Theology was the only class we were allowed to take and our time was to be spent in prayer and manual work. We canonicals cooked meals for all the other sisters and the students who lived in the dorm. Some days the kitchen looked like it was being run by a bunch of five year olds the way we bumped into each other and dropped utensils. We were not a very experienced group of cooks.

Five of us started out on the breakfast crew, which meant I raced out of chapel after Mass to help start the oatmeal, or toast, or whatever, while the rest of the Sisters chanted the morning Office. The rest of the day I was in the kitchen baking bread, frosting rolls, laying out bacon, and getting ready for the next morning. I developed my cooking skills much faster than my praying skills. We were allowed visitors three times the whole year: Christmas, Easter, and once in the fall. We could write a letter once a month and receive letters once a week. All in all, it was an emotionally stark year. I tried very hard to be a good little Sister of Mercy.

Because we weren't taking college classes and, theoretically, didn't need our sleep as much as the other sisters, we were assigned the privilege of keeping vigil during the night for a sister who had died. Barb and I were assigned the 3:00 A.M. hour with two other novices. Kneeling on a pew in a parlor at that time of the night, in silence, with candles flickering was asking for someone's imagination to take over. It did. A novice on the previous watch hid under the bier and made moaning sounds. Barb jumped and I stared bug-eyed. We looked at each other and then got brave enough to look behind the casket. After figuring out the moan was from a live person, we turned our attention to snooping around. We wanted to see if they buried the sisters with shoes. They did. The other two novices who were on watch gave us looks of disapproval for breaking the night silence. One of them was such a perfectionist she used to read a spiritual book while doing her charge of dusting in the chapel. We wondered if we were assigned the vigil hour with her so some of her compliance would rub off on us. Not a chance. We didn't have much influence on her, either.

Each of us had a feast day, depending on which saint our names represented. The name *Janice* came from *John* so I chose to honor St. John the Beloved, one of the apostles at the Last Supper who seemed like a nice guy to me. We no longer celebrated birthdays, at least officially, so our feast days became a substitute. Mine was on December 27, a lousy time of the year to get attention. It was January before anyone realized they had missed the date. Barb gave me a sewing booklet with instructions on how to make the habit. She attached a note saying I was now her seamstress. What about the last several years, Barb? The other sisters gave me a tray decorated with ribbon, medals of saints, holy cards, candy, and cartoons. I was used to minimal attention on my birthdays, but Barb was not. The day we both turned sixteen, I got a hairbrush. She got a grand piano and a party.

My enthusiasm for being in religious life, which had been at an all-time high during the summer, was pretty shot by February.

The Omaha weather didn't help with clouds, freezing temperatures, intense wind, and several feet of snow. I caught several chest colds which drained the life out of me. Since we weren't allowed to take naps, the coughs lingered for weeks.

We had regular classes with Mother Stan using a book called *The Constitution* which described how a Sister of Mercy was to live her life:

> *The Institute (of the Religious Sisters of Mercy) has for its GENERAL object the perfection of its members by the three simple Vows of Poverty, Chastity, and Obedience, and of these Constitutions. It has for its SPECIAL object the service of the poor, sick, and ignorant. The perfection of the religious soul depends not so much on performing extraordinary actions as on performing extraordinarily well the ordinary actions of every day. By performing all these actions well they shall perfect themselves, and their day shall be full of merit and good works.*

〜

We were expected to read a section from this book every day. We were expected to do a lot of things every day. Sometimes, we were so loaded down with work in the kitchen, the laundry room, and the sewing room we hardly had time for our required prayers and spiritual reading. If we didn't get them done, we had to tell Mother Stan, who was, of course, never pleased with our lack of organization.

The gray days of March and somberness of Lent brought out more pranks. For St. Patrick's Day, Barb and another novice dyed their hair (what little hair they had) green right before afternoon prayers. They ran short on time and had to put their coifs on before the food coloring dried. I couldn't keep custody of the eyes when they came into chapel with green dripping down their white guimpes. Pretty soon most of the novices were paying more attention to them than to their spiritual reading. Mother Stan had to tap her ring *and* clear her throat.

About that time, a novice had been told to leave. That scared me. The Council had decided she didn't belong because she wouldn't conform to all the rules and regulations. She would do unacceptable things like letting her veil fall back on her head instead of keeping it pulled forward to hide her face. Or, she would use colored plastic clothespins to pin her veil back while working in the kitchen. I liked her flair for individuality, but individuality had no place there. It was like boot camp.

Easter with all its candles, flowers, and food came as a huge relief after the barrenness of Lent which was a time of austerity in preparation for celebrating Easter. By then I was on the dinner crew which meant organizing the preparation of several twenty-pound turkeys, putting trays of rolls in the oven, preparing large bowls of salads, making huge pans of giblet gravy, and taking gallons of ice cream out of the freezer. The meal turned out great, much to my surprise, and not much food came back from the tables. During visiting time in the afternoon, Mom and Dad gave me a dozen colored eggs with many familiar drawings from childhood. I really knew it was Easter when I saw an egg with a familiar goofy portrait by Dad. I was touched by their sweet gestures.

⌐

Our group of novices was given the responsibility of leading the sisters in chanting the afternoon Office. Two of us would stand, walk to the large middle aisle, face the altar, genuflect, and start the chant in Latin so the rest of the sisters could answer. As luck would have it again, Barb and I were paired up for a week of leading the chant. One of the afternoons, I had been in the kitchen making biscuits and scooping flour from a waist-high trash can that was on wheels. The bell rang for Office and in my rush to get to the chapel I bumped into the trash can dumping white flour all over my black habit. I brushed frantically as I ran up the stairs to chapel while buttoning on my sleeves and trying to compose myself. According to later reports, I looked like Pigpen from *Peanuts* billowing a white cloud as I walked out to the middle aisle, genuflected, bowed, and started chanting. I caught a glimpse of Barb's startled face, and both of us immediately looked away. We knew better than to give in to laughter at a time like that.

The patron saint of kitchens was Saint Zita to whom we mumbled prayers almost constantly. She obviously wasn't paying attention when we made thirty-six lemon pies that wouldn't gel. Staring at them didn't help. I was the one who had read the recipe wrong from our *Betty Crocker Cookbook* so that we multiplied tablespoons of water instead of teaspoons. I tried to put the blame on my cohort but she was a math major and knew she hadn't made the error. We called the result "pie a la bowl" because we had to eat it with a spoon. Since the novitiate was expected to eat all the mistakes made in the kitchen, we had liquid lemon pie for days.

⌒

When I had been gone for about a year and a half, my family moved out of the only house I had ever known without telling me until much later. Of course, it was Marty who wrote to let me know. She was the only one who wrote regularly. The news hit me hard. I loved that house. It was colonial style and sat on a corner with huge cottonwood trees surrounding it. We had a white picket fence in the back, and Dad had always kept the yard green and decorated with flowers. He told me years later he was very, very sad having to leave a home with so many memories of us kids. But those memories were what tormented Mom and she thought a new house would help. Paul wrote one of his rare letters and enclosed a scribbled floor plan of the place. He said the whole family was excited about having a brand new home, especially one with more than one bathroom. I was happy for them but I felt so left out. Ironically, the house was in a newly developed area only about a mile from the convent.

One snowy, windy, cold Saturday afternoon I was in the kitchen peeling a huge pot of vegetables, staring out the window and thinking of how awful the winters were in Omaha. I was making up a story in my mind: "It was a dark and stormy night with the wind howling in the trees and the snow piling so deep that our poor heroine could barely see in front of her as she trudged painfully onward." I thought I was hallucinating when I saw the figure of a girl coming toward me in the snowstorm. It was my sister, Marty, plowing through the snow with her dog, Schotzy. She had not realized how bad the storm was when she left home to deliver her letter, knowing how I hated Saturdays without mail. We waved at each other. She looked so pitifully wet and cold, but I was not supposed to talk to her so I didn't. She walked around front, delivered the letter to the Sister at the reception area, and walked back home. I worried about her for hours after that. When I got the letter later that evening, I could hardly read it without crying. Why didn't I at least make sure she got warm before walking back home? I felt I was beginning not to think straight. Later she said no one in the front lobby noticed how cold she was so she turned around and left. She was not any better at asking for what she needed than I was.

Our first year as novices sped by and suddenly we were second-year novices. The good part was we did not have to work in the kitchen. I never did conquer the chaos of cooking for several hundred people. We were back in college and, once again, I was assigned education classes. Mother Provincial and the Council were very closed about what plans, if any, they had for me. I knew all along I wanted to be a nurse, but no one asked me. There were already several in my band who had some nursing education so I thought my chances were slim to none. The idea of teaching grade school didn't thrill me.

The time I questioned my vocation the most was New Year's Day, 1960. Barb and I had spent several hours the week before walking up the hill, talking about life, love, the pursuit of happiness and attempting to convince ourselves we should stay. We always did a lot of crying when we were in those moods. We were so tired of trying to be good. Some days I wanted to be a Bride of Christ and other days I just wanted to go home and be Anne Fangman again.

Anyway, when New Year's Eve came rolling around, some of "our gang" decided to liven up the night by having A PARTY. Never mind that we could get into trouble. We waited till the rest of the sisters were safely asleep. We snuck wine from the chapel sacristy, cookies and hot chocolate from the kitchen, and a radio from a hidden spot in the back of a storage closet. While *very* quietly groping in the dark stairwell next to the novitiate, I bumped into a wall and dropped an armful of plastic cups. All I could do was stare bug-eyed as they rolled merrily down the stairwell, clanking like cannons in the night silence. We held our breaths. Nobody came dashing out asking what was going on. Onward! The closer we got to the lounge on the college side (deserted because of Christmas break), the faster we walked. We flipped on lights, and turned on the radio to some dude blabbering about snowflakes as big as golf balls. Only it wasn't snowing where we were. It didn't dawn on us that the station was not local. As we poured our second glasses of wine, we concluded the DJ was probably drunk. Guy Lombardo came on from New York Times Square. We laughed, told stories, and felt wicked.

The morning after was awful. We couldn't stand the guilt we felt for doing the forbidden. Someone told us Mother Stan knew there were things going on the night before. Barb had decided she really was going home and had nothing to lose so she told Mother about the evening. During the course of the conversation, she realized Mother had absolutely no idea what Barb was talking about. Too late. Mother lectured each one of us individually about being a source of dis-edification for the others and how could we do such a thing, etc. Barb's taking the blame didn't help any. There was no humor in the situation this time. Each one of us anticipated being asked to leave because of our disobedience and it was almost a disappointment when we weren't. Once again Barb changed her mind about leaving and things settled down. I had too much fear and guilt to leave. I prayed and prayed and resolved to try some more.

We could always tell if a novice was thinking of leaving; she started letting her hair grow and usually had a hard time keeping it inside her coif. We were told not to discuss such thoughts with each other, although some of us did anyway. Mother Stan would say that when those thoughts came we were to pray about it. "It's just the devil tempting you, Sister." I let my hair grow several times, which, of course, was a long, slow process. Sometimes just the idea of leaving in the middle of a school semester and losing sixteen credit hours would motivate me to persevere to the end of the semester. Then, in a burst of fervor and/or fear, I would cut my hair short again. Besides, a lot of hair under all those layers of material was hot, even in the winter.

As the long winter moved into a gray March, Mother Stan noticed the novices and postulants getting restless and told some of us to organize a party for the rest of the novitiate. "Yes, Mother." We made up a skit about Romeo and Juliet, with a German accent:

> *Scene: Romeo enters stage left strumming a guitar while Juliet appears on the balcony (a ladder) combing her long hair (a mop).*
> *Juliet: Ah, Romeo, Romeo, I luv you mit all mine heart.*
> *Romeo: Ah, Juliet, mine luv, mit out you I vould die.*
> *Juliet: But, Romeo, vere have you ben vor so long?*
> *Romeo: Your, Fadder, he locked me in der valk-in freezer!*

And on and on. Another Novice imitated Jerry Lewis, conducting a chorus. Two others pretended they were first-graders, reading a poem in front of an audience, getting nervous, starting over, getting more nervous, starting over again, panicking, and ending up crying. The funniest skit was a novice mimicking the Maidenform Bra commercial, popular at the time, by waltzing onto the stage reciting "I dreamed I went to Ireland in my Erin Go Braugh." I don't think Mother Stan caught half of our jokes but she was right about us needing some laughs.

⌒

By summer, the convent was packed with sisters arriving from the other convents, some to attend summer school and some to take final vows in August. Many of us were anxious, not knowing if we would be allowed to make temporary vows. We joked about finding out we were not accepted by discovering our trunks on the back dock ready for pick up, the convent's version of the pink slip.

Barb and I didn't lose our knack for getting into trouble that summer. We just didn't do it as frequently. When we did, we often looked like a scene from a zany movie, chasing each other down a hall, ducking into a stairwell, and sliding down a banister. True to form, just as Barb would safely disappear, I would either lose my balance or stumble into a hallway and run smack-dab into an older Sister.

Never quite sure about us, Mother Stan called us into her office one afternoon to have a heart to heart. Barb and I sat next to each other on the hard-backed chairs, hands folded and feet on the floor, trying not to look at each other. "I've been watching the two of you for almost three years now, and I still don't know which one is the leader and which one is the follower." Intake of air. Hold breath. Exhale. "Yes, Mother." After leaving her office, we scrambled down the hall to get out of earshot.

"You be the leader today and I'll follow."

"Oh, no, dahling, you be the leader."

"Really, it's your turn."

Years later, we still can't agree on which one of us really was the leader and which one the follower. Another frustration Mother had with Barb and me was trying to figure out if we had a "Particular Friendship" (or P.F. as we called it in the novitiate). She kept warning the novices and postulants against natural friendships "as they may be foolish, sentimental, or sensual in character." Barb and I would look at each other and say, "Does she think we're physically attracted to each other?" If there were physical attractions going on between Sisters, I was oblivious. Two Sisters seen frequently in each others' company would be reprimanded for not socializing equally with the other Sisters. Barb and I figured if we had a P.F. we'd had it since fifth grade, for heaven's sake. We just ignored Mother Stan when she started on the topic and figured she was lecturing the group about someone else. We would later lock arms and sing:

Oh, we ain't got a barrel of money.
Maybe we're ragged and funny.
But we'll travel along,
Singing our song,
Side by side.

Barb and Anne, 1961

JUNIORATE

Much to our amazement, both Barb and I were accepted for temporary vows. The ceremony was less emotional than the one for reception of the habit, but still beautiful. The black veil replaced the white novice veil, and we pronounced the vows of poverty, chastity, and obedience as a group, inserting our individual names:

In the name of our Lord and Savior, Jesus Christ, and under the protection of His Immaculate Mother, Mary ever Virgin, I, Anne Marie Fangman, called in Religion, Sister Mary Janice, do vow and promise to God, Poverty, Chastity, and Obedience and the service of the poor, sick and ignorant and to persevere for three years in this Institute of Our Lady of Mercy, according to its Constitutions in the presence of you, Mother Provincial, delegate of Mother General of the Religious Sisters of Mercy of the Union in the United States of America, this 16th day of August in the year of our Lord, 1960.

Along with making the vows, we transitioned to living in the Juniorate which was one floor below the Novitiate. Wearing the black veil and being a Junior Professed sister felt very adult. We had visitors again that day and, according to Marty, we looked like "real Nuns." Except for the absence of a silver wedding band, we did look like the final product. The Council had recently changed the number of years from three to five before we could take final vows and receive a wedding band. We figured they looked at our group and decided we needed those extra two years to grow up. If a sister decided to leave after final vows, she would need a dispensation from the Pope. I had never heard of anyone doing that. In fact, I had never heard of anyone leaving voluntarily after taking temporary vows. Little did I know I would be the first one.

⌒

Being a Junior Professed did not calm my spirit for long. I went into a period of fantasizing about working in Laos with Dr. Tom Dooley after reading his book, *The Night They Burned the Mountain*. Not only did I get jazzed about saving the world, I became enamored of him, imagining what it would be like to be with someone so compassionate, sensitive, and good-looking. As I fell asleep, I'd imagine being held and loved by someone like him. I ached for it. I cried about it.

I had no one to talk with about my feelings except for Barb and she was usually more depressed than I was. Everyone else would say, "Pray about it, Sister," or, "The devil is just tempting you." Others thought I was such a good Sister of Mercy and I kept praying that my exterior compliance would develop into inner conviction. God seemed so far away. I had been convinced that, as long as the Sisters of Mercy accepted me, I had a vocation, that it was not my decision. I had heard that said so many times and had read similar statements in spiritual reading books I was convinced it was the truth. Theoretically, the three things necessary for a vocation to the religious life were: health, intelligence, and desire. The desire was my weak spot.

During the eight years I was in the convent, I never quite settled into being there. The emotional storms came and went. Sometimes I thought I was content to be where I was, and other times I was totally confused. I thought I did too much thinking. The restrictions on what we could read and not read had been relaxed once we were out of the novitiate and we were allowed to check out classics from the college library. I loved to read and was like a kid in a candy store. One of the classics I chose was *Lady Chatterleys' Lover*. I didn't feel guilty about reading it; I felt fascinated. The concept of sex being beautiful and not shameful made me even more envious of those who could experience it. But that wasn't what I was on this earth for, right? I begged God for help. I also read a book by St. Theresa who said that God comes to the convent to find peace instead of the nagging complaints of his friends in the world. So then I would feel guilty about begging for clarity. My thoughts were going in circles.

During March my old flame, Patrick, showed up with some other Jesuit seminarians to participate in a student body panel discussion about vocations in the religious life. Those of us who had known the seminarians were allowed to visit in a parlor afterward where we laughed and told stories on each other. Afterward, I walked Patrick to his car. (Seminarians had the privilege of driving and going places alone!) As I stood there, smothered in black and starch, chatting with him, I had a twinge of the old familiar attraction. Almost in slow motion, I watched him take off his black jacket, hook it on his finger and throw it over his shoulder while he casually chatted away. I knew I wasn't dead yet. I flashed on being married, having children, looking up recipes in the *Betty Crocker Cookbook* and not having to multiply them by 100.

I spent many hours sitting in chapel and praying or walking outside to meditate on what my life was *supposed* to be. In the Juniorate our Mistress of Juniors, Sister Mary Cecilia, was the total opposite of Mother Stanislaus. We didn't even have to call her Mother. She smiled instead of frowned and had a sense of humor she was glad to share with us. She did have a much easier job since we were already molded into good Sisters of Mercy. Being Irish, she personified their classic charm and warmth. She was also determined to teach me to crochet. "You need to learn something that will occupy your hands when you get old, my dear." I liked her so much I tried to learn, sometimes using our time together to talk about my struggles. She was always very pleasant but would give the standard line of, "You are such a good little Sister; pray about it, dear." Pray! Again! So I would go pray.

School became increasingly difficult. I was in anatomy and physiology class, which meant there was hope I might be heading to nursing school. That was the good part. The bad part was the teacher mumbled, and I was having trouble passing the weekly quizzes. For the life of me, I could not remember the twelve cranial nerves, even with several catchy memory rhymes to help. However, I immediately memorized and never forgot a silly backwards version of "Cinderella and the Prince" called:

PRINDERELLA AND THE CINCE

Tonce upon a wime, there was a gretty little pirl named Prinderella. She had two sisty uglers and a micked stepwother who made her wean the clindows, pine the shots and shans and do all the other wirty dork. Wasn't that a shirty dame?

One day the Ping issued a kroclomation that all geligible irls were to attend the drancy fess ball. But Prinderella couldn't go. She didn't have a drancy fess. All she had was a rirty dag. That fidn't dit. Wasn't that a shirty dame?

BUT, Prinderella's Gairy Fodmother came to the rescue. She made the hice into morses, the cumpkin into a poach, and the rirty dag into a drancy fess and told Prinderella to be home by the moke of stridnight.

So, Prinderella went to the drancy fess ball and pranced with the Cince all night. Then, at the moke of stridnight, as Prinderella was running down the stalace peps, on the bottom pep she slopped her dripper!

The next day, the Ping issued another kroclomation that all geligible irls were to sly on the dripper. Prinderella's two sisty uglers slied on the dripper, but it fidn't dit. But Prinderella slied on the dripper and it fid dit! So, Prinderella and the Cince hived lappily ever after. That wasn't such a shirty dame, was it?

⌣

Speech was another one of my classes I was ambivalent about. I loved getting in front of an audience, but I got very nervous. The most fun presentation I had was a Personal Experience talk about a high school adventure of hounding Dean Martin and Jerry Lewis for autographs (in the days before stars had much security surrounding them):

Several of us, with Barb in the lead (according to my version), tracked down where Martin and Lewis were staying while they performed in Omaha. We took the hotel elevator, bravely walked down the hall, and knocked on the door. Jerry Lewis himself answered! We stood there gawking. He broke the silence by slamming the door in our faces. We were so startled we didn't move. Suddenly, a second door opened down the hall, and there he was making faces at us. After getting us to run back and forth between doors a few times, he let us in and politely signed autographs. When he was not being goofy, he was actually nice looking. Then, he asked if we wanted to see Dean. Is the Pope Catholic? We followed him up a flight of stairs, during which he would go up two and back one, bumping us all into peals of laughter. He led us right into Dean Martin's bedroom! There he was, lying on the bed singing along with the radio. Mr. Lewis disappeared and we very politely asked for autographs. Mr. Martin wasn't too happy we were there but tried to be pleasant and we rewarded him by gushing and swooning. As he was writing on the scraps of paper we handed him some of us snuck cigarette butts from the ashtray and then backed out of the room saying, "Thank you!" We surmised the two of them later exchanged a few heated words about the situation. We, however, had a grand time.

⌐

School dragged along. In addition to a heavy class load, I was assigned to drive other Sisters to off-campus classes and appointments; I was one of the few who had a driver's license left over from high school days and knew the city. One afternoon, the only available car was a stick shift which I had never learned to drive. The Sister who was my companion knew how but had no license. She coached me as I chugged up and down the hills of Omaha. I ran a red light, slammed on the brakes at another light, and almost backed into a car as I tried to get out of the intersection. I would not recommend that form of driver education.

Back in the Juniorate Sister Mary Cecilia had weekly classes with us regarding the vows of poverty, chastity, and obedience. Again, we used *The Constitution of the Sisters of Mercy:*

POVERTY: *We are to own nothing. Whatever we use is for that, our use. We are to be willing to give up anything at any moment; which is why we say "our" shoes, "our" bed, "our" stationary, etc. If we are given a gift, we must ask permission to keep it; if we earn a salary, we must put it in the common fund. The chapel is to be the only part of the convent to be as richly decorated as possible to exemplify that our resources are to be used for the honor and glory of God, not our own.*

CHASTITY: *We are to love no one in any sexual way. We are to be accommodating, kind, sympathetic and cordial, but in a non-sensual manner. The Customs and Guide directs us to regulate the manner of walking and gesturing to symbolize that God is the end of our thoughts and desires. When leaving the premises of the convent, we are to do so with the permission of the superior, travel with a companion, and arrive home before dark.*

OBEDIENCE: *We are not to have a will of our own. The Constitution reminds the sisters to "bear in mind that by the Vow of Obedience they have, to a certain extent, renounced their wills, resigning them to the direction of their superiors. They are to obey their superiors as holding their authority from God. We are not to question about assignments.*

⌒

The vow that bothered me the most was the vow of chastity because I didn't think I'd ever be completely detached from my need for human love. I wasn't good at keeping custody of the eyes, either, especially when there was a good-looking man in the vicinity. In the novitiate, Mother Stanislaus had said, "Don't feel upset or guilty about sexual dreams; you have no control over them. Just don't dwell on them while awake. And most of all never touch your private parts." Huh?

The vow that bothered me the least was poverty. I hadn't owned much of anything up to that point and didn't have much to give up. It was more of an irritation than a major challenge to call everything "our." And, so far, the vow of obedience wasn't terribly difficult. I had been used to being obedient to my parents and teachers. Some of the older Sisters had a hard time accepting a change of assignment from where they would teach or nurse because they had grown used to where they had been and liked the people. I was sure I would have more than one opportunity down the road to remind myself that I had taken a vow of obedience.

At that point in my life I had very little self-awareness of who I was as an individual so any feedback was an eye-opener for me. One of the sisters was into handwriting analysis and agreed to do mine. Most of her interpretation was encouraging, but there were a few statements that gave me pause: "Circumstances might force you to comply with rules or another's decisions; but, many times, you would prefer not to. You don't show enthusiasm, but do a job out of determination." Did I? That's not how I wanted to live. What really made me wonder were the statements, "You like to act on your own," and, "Your personal appearance and manner is of great concern."

About that time, another Sister started on a crusade to find out what made me tick. She was a person who felt it was her duty to know everyone elses' business and that made me not want to tell her anything. It bugged her that I wouldn't pour out my most personal thoughts to her. She was right about one thing, though;

I did keep my deepest feelings hidden. In spite of all the talking Barb and I did, there was a lot we didn't share because neither one of us knew how. As I was growing up, nobody in my family talked about feelings. Instead, the message was to be quiet and comply. As a toddler, according to family stories, I had quite a temper. One time, I suspect I was mad about being bumped off my pedestal by the arrival of my younger brother, Paul. In a fit of frustration, I threw his baby bottle shattering the huge mirror in back of the sofa. That was one of many times Mom sent me to the hall closet with the door shut for punishment. I would sit on the vacuum in the dark and cry, eventually being allowed to come out when I promised to be good. I grew up having an aversion to vacuums.

The early sixties were a time of animated discussion among the Sisters of Mercy about how to comply with the recommendation of Pope John XXIII. He had convened the Second Vatican Council to bring "a breath of fresh air" into the church resulting in a lot of unanswered questions about how to do that. One topic of the Vatican Council encouraged religious orders to renew the simplicity of their founders and get rid of burdensome customs and practices and bring themselves into the present. As a result, representatives of the Sisters of Mercy from all over the United States gathered in Atlanta to plan for the future of the order. Our Mistress of Juniors, Sister Mary Cecilia, attended and when she returned gave us an enthusiastic summary of the meetings. She said hours had been spent debating the habit which had not changed since Mother McAuley founded the order in Ireland in 1831. Many of the older sisters got pretty riled saying they would never wear a modern habit no matter what the General Council decided. The idea of their ankles showing brought exclamations of "immodest!" They also panicked about having their gray hair and wrinkles on display. I hadn't worn the habit for fifty years and I had no wrinkles or gray hair to hide, but I didn't think we had much choice. We were not supposed to have vanity about our looks but I knew most of us did.

Not only did I struggle emotionally most of the time; I also struggled physically. After fighting colds, sore throats, and severe coughs for years, I had my tonsils out at the ripe young age of twenty-one. After surgery the nurses couldn't get me to wake up; they begged, pleaded, cajoled, and bribed but I snoozed away. The combination of anesthetic, pain medications, and total exhaustion were enough to keep me in a deep sleep. Barb stayed at my bedside the morning of surgery and my family was there the rest of the day. I would wake up long enough to mumble something and then crash again. Marty said I looked stunning in my night coif which was constantly falling over my eyes.

"Why do you wear that stupid thing, anyway?"

"We have to wear something on our heads at all times. Modesty, you know."

"You gotta be kidding."

Being a patient in the hospital as an adult was a whole lot easier than being a patient when I was six years old. At least this time I knew why I was there. When I finally did wake up enough to go back to the convent my throat was incredibly sore, but at least I could enjoy the luxury of staying in bed and reading some good books. The other Sisters brought me meals and ice packs for my neck. All the attention felt awkward, but I adapted and soon was soaking it up.

Before surgery, I had been taking voice lessons. I think Sister Mary Cecilia encouraged me to take them to give me some pleasant distraction because she knew how much I liked to sing. I was hoping that going to the hospital would get me out of the recital, but no such luck. The music instructor postponed it so I could have the dubious honor of standing in front of an audience of Sisters while timidly singing some song. Not that I minded performing; I just minded the idea of a recital. It didn't help my confidence that several other Sisters in the recital had incredible talent.

Music was part of our culture. On balmy summer evenings we would go outside and have a songfest, recently re-named a hootenanny. Some of the Sisters who were teachers had obtained the words to *Michael Row the Boat Ashore, Where Have all the Flowers Gone?* and several Peter, Paul and Mary songs. Many of the Sisters could harmonize easily; I usually stuck to the main tune and didn't try anything fancy.

Summer was not all about singing. I was assigned to take

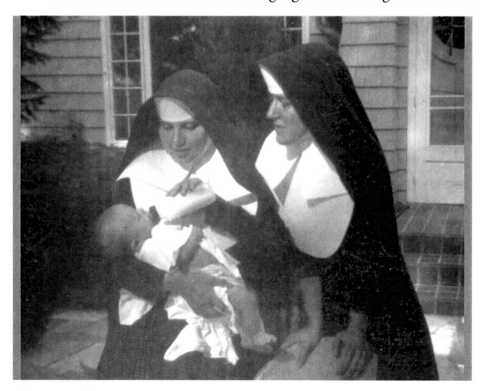

Barb and Anne with former nun's baby.

my annual retreat in June so I could help with the behind-the-scenes cooking, cleaning, and answering phones while the other Sisters had their retreat in August. My retreat was at Mercy high school with the Sisters who lived there. I spent one evening wandering around the classrooms. At every door, a flood of high school memories would hit me and I became aware of how strange I felt walking the halls as an official Sister of Mercy instead of an immature student. I had thought going back to my alma mater would bring feelings of warmth. Instead, I felt lost, like I didn't belong. By the end of the eight days of silence I was wound up and ready to climb the walls. I would laugh at anything, even the retreat master's new haircut. This time I didn't have a buddy to share the humor and help me get into trouble. I wondered if this is how I would feel when I got sent to a smaller convent.

The retreat was in the same chapel as the three-day retreat I had made as a senior, ages ago, when I decided to give the convent a try. The retreat master gave us Sisters an interesting talk on chastity. Or maybe I just woke up for that one. He seemed to be saying, in his vague way, that having problems with chastity was normal. I prayed for the grace to want the life of a Sister of Mercy.

Around July the excitement about the coming year's appointments became intense. Rumors had been going around for days that assignments would be posted any minute. Most of my group would continue at the college to finish their studies but we were excited about where our buddies in the other bands were going. There was still no decision about my starting nursing school. The other option for me was to do student teaching and then be a grade school teacher which I would have to accept gracefully. I would also have to revive our novitiate saying of, *Thank You God. Dang it.*

Our band gave a going-away party with skits for the two bands ahead of us and in return they gave us a party with more skits. After the second party we had been re-hashing the skits when the bell rang for night prayers, which meant instant silence. It wasn't easy chopping off a punch line in mid-sentence, and we snickered all the way to chapel.

On August 18, 1961, Barb and I turned twenty-two. Barb's Mom brought a cake for us and Sister Mary Cecilia was kind enough to let us have a nice little party. During that year, Barb and I had spent long periods of time without seeing much of each other and, true friends that we were, would drift back together picking up where we had left off without missing a beat.

I was spending a good deal of time working in the rose garden and had begun to think of it as my garden. Since no one had taken a previous interest in the garden, it had become run down. When I told Mom and Dad about enjoying the garden they brought over two rose bushes and a trellis. Just when I got the place shaped-up, one of the other Sisters was assigned to it as her charge. I tried to be philosophical, telling myself it was hot work outside. But I had loved working with the roses and missed the joy of tending to something alive. I thought it was a mean gesture to take it away from me but what could I do? Obedience raised its cranky head.

⤳ NURSING SCHOOL ⤳

The Provincial Council finally decided to send Sister Robert Mary, another junior sister, and me to the four-year baccalaureate nursing program at Creighton, a Jesuit University in Omaha. In the past, all the sisters had gone to one of the three-year diploma program run by the Sisters of Mercy. I didn't care where I went to school; I just wanted to be a nurse! Sister Robert Mary and I were so excited we didn't miss a beat starting to make the all-white habits for nursing uniforms. We spent our two-week Christmas break in a crash course, Introduction to Nursing, so we could be up to speed with our sophomore class by the time we joined them in February. We squeezed into our teacher's (one of the Sisters who was a nurse) tiny office with a coffee pot and some munchies. Sister Robert Mary quipped, "This is the only class I know that starts with The Grace before Meals." She could be very witty and, at that time, I was glad to be partnered with her.

We both started diaries and addressed them "Dear, Phoebe" because "Dear Diary" sounded boring. Phoebe had been a nurse-type person during the time of St. Paul, a piece of useless information we picked up in class. If anyone had read our diaries they would've been hard pressed to prove we were going to the same school together. We experienced things very differently. Sister Robert Mary, in spite of her sense of humor, turned out to be a very intense person. I could be serious, but not *that* serious.

We visited the Creighton campus to get a textbook for our class on marriage. Yes, Religious Sisters of Mercy would be taking a class on marriage. Even stranger, a priest would be teaching the course. In theory, we needed to know the church's philosophy on marriage and some of the problems of marriage. O.K., we could understand that. Our vow of poverty allowed us to purchase only one text for each of our classes. We were to share and then pass the book on to the Sisters who would be taking the class next year. Our visit to the campus was the first time Sister Robert Mary had been to Creighton. It was definitely not my first time. In high school, Barb and I used to haunt Creighton's dances, checking out the older men. They didn't look older any more.

We soon figured out the difference between a college and a university: it took twenty minutes to register at the College of Saint Mary. It took three hours to register at Creighton University. The process was baffling. I wasn't used to being surrounded by people, people, and more people, especially men. Most of them were so courteous and helpful I felt like a little old lady trying to cross the street. Since it was 1962 and smoking was permitted everywhere, I spent much of the time choking on pipe and cigarette smoke. I wondered if it helped students to puff away while filling out forms.

We stood in line for at least fifteen minutes before someone could take our registration cards, mumble that they were filled out correctly, and point us to the next line. At the College of St. Mary we were considered seniors. At Creighton we were listed as juniors but we were taking nursing classes with sophomores. We felt like freshmen.

Sister Robert Mary faced the semester with "fear and trembling because of the responsibility we have to represent the Sisters of Mercy." I was just looking forward to learning and I told her so. Her retort was, "You always were an idiot, Fangman." (She usually called me Fangman when we were alone.) She made these comments as if she were joking but underneath there was real sarcasm. I was taken aback by many of the things she said to me.

When the first day of class arrived, I did find myself a bit nervous at the newness of it all. It helped that the other nursing students went out of their way to welcome us. In the free time between classes, Sister Robert Mary and I would sit in a pew of the big old St. John Church trying to say our prayers. I say trying because we were distracted by the antics of this little old man who was cleaning. He would rush around dragging his vacuum and mumbling every time it fell over. We expected him to break into, "I'm late, I'm late for a very important date. No time to say, 'hello, good-bye,' I'm late, I'm late, I'm late!" Sister Robert Mary called Creighton the Dust Bowl because we were forever wiping dust from the bottom of our black habits. Sitting in a classroom chair took courage, knowing we would be "marked women" when we stood up. Those Jesuits needed a little training from Mother Stanislaus on how to clean.

In those days there was a convent across the street from the Creighton administration building for our Sisters who taught at St.

John's grade school, also located across the street. We would walk over for lunch and experience a taste of life in a small convent. The superior showed us where the peanut butter was kept in case we got hungry. We were in heaven. We had never before been allowed to go to the kitchen and fix something to eat between meals. We wished we could live there to make our commute to school easier. No way. We were still considered in spiritual development which meant living with the rest of the junior sisters and being closely supervised.

With a three-year hospital based nursing program, students would take their patient care experiences in one hospital. But with our relatively new four-year program, we took our clinical experiences, or rotations, in various hospitals. Our medical-surgical experience was at Saint Joseph's Hospital run by a different group of sisters. It was the hospital where I was born, was briefly a patient at age thirteen, and worked as a nursing assistant. Now I would gather more history there. We were not allowed to wear our white habits on Creighton's campus. They just *might* get dirty. So we had to change at the hospital which involved maneuvering in a tiny tub room with no place to hang our black habits. Superman had more elbowroom in his phone booth. During our first morning as nursing students we learned how to make a bed, hospital-style, with mitered corners and sheets tight enough to spin a quarter on them. After Mother Stan's training, this was a piece of cake.

It was winter and the early morning commute soon became a drag. Icy roads caused us to take an hour instead of the usual twenty minutes to get to the hospital and once we got there, we had to hit the deck running. Giving my first bed bath was no small challenge. We had learned in class what seemed like a hundred steps to giving a bath to a patient in bed. I couldn't remember what step to do next. Start at the top and work down?... stop in the middle?... front to back?... back to front?... side to side?... How do I untangle the bath blanket? Keeping up a coherent conversation at the same time was almost impossible. My patient was a woman who wasn't very sick but volunteered to stay in bed so I could practice on her. I started to relax when I realized she was enjoying herself. She was not Catholic so had several questions about sisters and thought I was "just the type to be a Nun." I controlled my urge to make up a story about a tragic love affair that caused me to give up the world and enter a nunnery.

Back on campus, the Jesuit who taught our philosophy class would shout at the students in an effort to keep us on our toes or at least awake after lunch. One day, the student sitting next to me kept asking me for the answers. The teacher eventually called on her then bowed to me saying, "Thank you for the correct answer, Sister Janice." The class cracked up. This teacher also had the habit of repeating half a word until someone finished it, like defi... defi... defi... (for definition) or indi... indi... indi... (for individuating). My mind had a way of picking up on things like that. I started saying thera... thera . . .thera... for therapeutic nursing.

By March, we worked in a newer part of the hospital where they had running water in each room. In the old wing, we had to walk down a long hall to the utility room to fill a pitcher with hot water, but by the time we got it back to the patient the water was lukewarm. Then we would rush back down the hall for rinse water, leaving the patient shivering under a thin bath blanket. One morning both of my patients were men and I couldn't tell what they thought of having a Sister take care of them. Luckily, one of them was gone most of the morning to x-ray and the other wandered the halls with his wife. I could see why he had high blood pressure; his wife talked constantly. He kept telling her to shut up and then turning to me to apologize for his language.

Eventually, spring arrived and life was worth living again. No more slush, shawls, or sweaters. Dodging the crazy drivers on campus was difficult enough without avoiding splashes of melting snow. Several times the wind blew our veils over our heads and with arms full of books we looked anything but dignified.

The main thing I worried about was passing pharmacology class. Our instructor was as tough as a drill sergeant. The more I studied, the more nervous I became, the more quizzes I would blow, and the more I would study. It was awful. I got an F at the quarter. I'd never gotten an F before. I absolutely had to pass pharmacology before I could continue in nursing. As Sister Robert Mary put it, "We've shed more tears over that class than all our sins put together." But she wasn't failing!

Barb tried to make light of the situation. She gave me a book of salad recipes, "Just in case you flunk out of nursing and wind up in the kitchen." I had a hard time laughing about it. She was studying to be an elementary school teacher back at the College of Saint Mary so we didn't see each other very often, and I missed being able to share everything with her.

When Sister Robert Mary and I were working the hospital we had many times of high anxiety. Giving the dreaded first injection was one of those times for most of the class. We practiced on oranges for a week, but I was shaking so much I thought I would stab a patient to death just trying. Charting was another anxiety-provoking task. I was in such a rush one morning I almost charted in the wrong chart. The fear of God had been put in us about checking and re-checking everything we did. I was sure I was going to make some terrible mistake and be banned from nursing.

Thankfully, the exam at the end of the semester was true-false with best guess answers. As Sister Robert Mary said before the test,

"Don't think, Fangman, just remember."

The philosophy exam was a snap; I had taken so many philosophy classes when I was in the Novitiate, I could make up answers. The best part of the end of the semester was learning I had passed pharmacology. As Sister Robert Mary and I were walking out of the administration building the last day of exams, our pharmacology instructor yelled from across the street:

"Hey, Sister Janice, you passed!"

"Who, me?"

"Ya, you got a B for your final grade. Congratulations!"

"I could hug you."

"Control yourself!"

⌒

Before we had time to catch our breaths, summer school started with medical-surgical classes all day Mondays on campus. We packed lunches, gobbling them down in the Sisters' lounge in the library. I swore I was going to name my book (the one I was always threatening to write) *Mustard Every Monday* because our sandwiches were usually ham and mustard. Eight hours of lecture left me glassy-eyed and I could not remember one thing the instructor said after lunch. I was convinced I had slept through the afternoon.

When Sister Robert Mary and I were working in the hospital our days were in lock step. In order to get to the hospital and be ready for work by 7:00 A.M., we had to be up before anyone else in the convent. Sister Robert Mary took on the task of waking me and would call in a stage whisper, "Annie, Annie." I'd bolt upright expecting her to say, "Get your gun!" That was the only time she ever called me Annie. We had a pact: don't remember anything said to each other before 10:00 A.M. It took that long for my brain to start functioning. We would drive to the hospital in relative silence, go to Mass with the sisters there, get our breakfast in the hospital cafeteria, and eat in a little room at the back of the cafeteria. By this point we had been assigned a bedroom behind the chapel for changing into our white habits. It was nice and private. Too private. We accidentally locked ourselves in there one morning and had to pound on the door to be noticed, probably disturbing all the Franciscan Sisters meditating in the chapel. A little old Sister finally let us out, tsk tsk-ing at us.

By July we were taking care of gynecology patients. One of my patients had beautiful brown hair that reached below her hips and I would comb and braid it for her. It was such a treat for me to comb hair, a far cry from scratching stubble. Another patient talked my leg off. "It doesn't make any difference to you that I'm not a Catholic, does it? Now does it? Really? You'd tell me, wouldn't you? You look like you'd be honest."

Even though the hospital was run by a group of Sisters, the patients and staff were not used to seeing young Sisters as students. Everywhere we went and everything we did was noticed, or so it seemed. Why are you here and not at the hospital run by your Sisters? You're so young and pretty, why are you in a convent? Do Sisters really do patient care?

Sometimes things would get tense between the Creighton students and the staff nurses. Most of the staff were graduates from the hospital's three-year school of nursing. Some of them became openly hostile about our type of education saying we had "too much book-learning and not enough practical experience." To that, I would say, "I just want to be a good nurse, no matter what type of education I get." I didn't know what else to say. I didn't feel like arguing with them. Other nurses would act indifferently, while some gave us encouragement.

Interactions between Sister Robert Mary and me became tense. She didn't even approve of the way I drove. When I got a ticket for parking smack-dab in front of a no parking sign on campus, I just laughed. She got irritated that I hadn't noticed the sign. She also said I wasn't paying attention to important things like the politics in the nursing department. One minute she would act as if she were my best friend and the next minute wouldn't speak to me. She was such a bright, witty person, there were times I thought she was right and I was, indeed, a dummy. My self-confidence would plunge and I felt I'd never be a good nurse. I was having enough stress getting through school without coping with her mood swings. Once again, there wasn't anyone I could talk to. I didn't have enough information at the time to realize there might have been something bothering her that she was taking out on me.

By August the appointments for the following year were posted at the Motherhouse. Sister Robert Mary and I were assigned to live at the convent across the street from Creighton. Finally! We were afraid they were going to make us commute for another year.

It took us only two and a half hours to register for classes the second time. Sister Robert Mary and I were to take a philosophy class together; but, as I was standing in line to get my schedule checked, the class filled up. I was relieved to have an excuse to sign up for something else. Not having all my classes with her would give me less exposure to her pointed sarcasm.

～

Our class schedules turned out to be less busy than we had anticipated which was good since our clinical hours in surgery consumed a big chunk of time. The surgery experience started with practicing scrubbing, gowning, and gloving, so we would be safe to be in the operating rooms. Our instructor was so nervous she made us nervous. We kept contaminating ourselves by accidentally bumping into things, which meant starting the process all over again until we could do it right. We were afraid to breathe and were walking around stiff as robots. Our class clown came to the rescue. After she was completely scrubbed, gowned and gloved, she walked over to the instructor, gave her a big hug, and said, "Bam, you're contaminated!" We all laughed so hard the instructor had to join in.

Community regulations would not allow Sisters to remove any part of the habit (except for the starched guimpe in front) while scrubbing for surgery. It was a huge challenge to cover everything with sterile gowns, gloves, caps, and booties. I felt and looked like an overstuffed mummy waddling around the operating room. It was hot under all those layers, especially with the operating room lights and tension heating up the room.

During my second day of experience, I scrubbed for surgery on a woman having a mastectomy. I got so engrossed in the procedure I practically pushed the surgeon out of the way. He was unusually patient with my questions. (Surgeons are not exactly known for their patience.) I knew, in spite of my enthusiasm to learn, I didn't want to work in surgery in the future. Anesthetized patients weren't very good at conversation.

Surgeons loved to tease nursing students, and we tried to give them a hard time back. One of the students fell for an old line when a surgeon told her to "hurry to sterile supply and get me a fallopian tube." She was halfway there when she remembered a fallopian tube is part of the female anatomy and not something to run and get. By the time she got back to the operating room, she was ready to kill the surgeon who was still laughing.

In spite of being a stressful time, the six weeks of surgery went quickly. It took a toll on me, though. I would wake up each morning with stomach pain, convinced I was developing an ulcer from the pressure of working in surgery and living with Sister Robert Mary. I could never predict whether she would be friend or foe.

Our exam for surgery was easy and I pulled an A. The instructor liked the papers I wrote and, during my last conference with her, said I had a talent for writing. I could hardly look at her, though, without laughing because of an incident that had happened in class. She had been lecturing about therapeutic this, therapeutic that. "The care for your patients should always be therapeutic. Your medications are therapeutic; your treatments are therapeutic," blah, blah, blah. I whispered to the student next to me, "She's so uptight. What she needs is a good therapeutic screw!" Well, that spread through the classroom like wildfire. "Did you hear what Sister Janice just said?" We shortened Good Therapeutic Screw to GTS for use in public. Every once in a while one of the students would say, "Boy, I could use a GTS."

Our ophthalmology experience was on a unit supervised by one of the Sisters who ran the hospital. I could feel her influence; it was the coziest, nicest, most efficient floor in the hospital. Everything was where it was supposed to be and the staff seemed calmer. I hoped I would have the same effect on my floors in the future.

The week we were scheduled for orthopedic experience, I had a bad chest cold and couldn't work. I said at the time, "Watch, I'll probably be assigned to work in orthopedics when I graduate." Sure enough, it did happen.

⌒

Each time we made it through another semester, Sister Robert Mary repeated our motto, "We came. We bluffed. We graduated." Our obstetric rotation was in the hospital run by our Sisters of Mercy. We had the luxury of living there for the three months instead of at the convent on campus which meant a lot less commute time. Our instructor had a thick Texas accent which I picked up without realizing it. After a particularly long day in class I was saying "y'all," "y'hear," and "hun."

In spite of my efforts to keep my sense of humor, there were days when nothing was funny at all. As we went through different rotations, learning to face suffering patients was difficult. I hardly wrote in my journal. I didn't have the energy for it. Sister Robert Mary and I drifted further apart even though we were together every day doing our pediatric and then our public health experiences. She developed some medical problems and was also getting psychological counseling once a week. I prayed something would help her. She seemed so unhappy and would hardly speak to me. She had to drop out for a semester, so I took my psychiatry rotation without her, much to my relief.

Those three months of being in Psychiatry changed my life. It turned out to be my favorite rotation, mainly because I learned so much about myself. For the first time in my life, I realized that everyone has anger, fear, frustrations, and needs. Life is supposed to be learning how to deal with feelings, not just suppressing or ignoring them. I learned I didn't have to be perfect! In fact, it wasn't healthy to expect that.

The most important new concept for me was personal accountability, being responsible for my own feelings and decisions. It did not mean I shouldn't listen to authority. It just meant I couldn't abdicate the responsibility of my life to others. That information scared me. I watched one of my patients curl up in the corner of her room unwilling to talk. Her history indicated she was not willing to accept responsibility for her own life and wanted decisions made for her. I looked at her and thought, "Is that me down the road? Am I unwilling to make my own decisions about my life?"

I had not thought much about my vocation since starting nursing school because school was so distracting. I realized then I had a lot more thinking to do. I needed to figure out what my values were, not the values of my parents, or my superiors, or even Sister Robert Mary. A religious group did not run the hospital where we were taking our psych experience and none of the lectures had the overlay of religion. For the first time in my life I was in the midst of secular learning and found it fascinating. There was nothing said that contradicted what I had learned previously, it just felt more worldly. I felt myself expanding and maturing with information about how the psyche works and how we as humans carry our childhood into adulthood. I took the first step of looking at my family members and how they influenced who I had become. I got so busy wrapping up the school year I did not pursue those thoughts, tucking them away for future exploration.

School ended, I graduated, and I was back at the Motherhouse with the rest of my band. Every once in a while, we had a chance to enjoy the summer. A physician had given the Sisters of Mercy a secluded cabin on a lake. We called it Mercy Acres. The junior Sisters were allowed to go swimming one afternoon. I have no idea where we obtained all those bathing suits, but there we were romping around in the water. With all the rules, though, it was a challenge to relax. Bathing caps were to be worn at all times. We were not to lie around in the sun but had to put on our long, black bathrobes as soon as we got out of the water. On hindsight, it was probably a good thing we couldn't lie in the sun; all those black clothes on top of sunburn would have been awful. Most of us stayed in the water and played. It felt so good to have the water and sun and air on my skin.

However, the summer was anything but fun and games. I was assigned to work as a Graduate Nurse in a hospital the Sisters of Mercy had recently converted into a nursing home. I couldn't work as a Registered Nurse until I passed State Boards later that summer. Working in geriatrics turned out to be frustrating. We were so understaffed and disorganized that my days were spent racing. I was starting IVs on old folks and hardly knew what I was doing. Passing medications took me way too long, not only because I was new at it but also because old folks take forever swallowing pills... one... at... a... time and ask what each pill is.

Omaha weather that time of the year could be 90 degrees and 90% humidity but the patients complained of being cold, so the air conditioning was turned off. The place felt like a steam bath. Many of the patients were senile, bedridden, and badly in need of human contact. I wanted to spend more time touching and comforting but I didn't have the time. The moaning, the diarrhea, the bedpans all got to me and by the end of the day, I felt like crying. I was in over my head. The whole idea of a four-year nursing program was to graduate a flexible, mature nurse with leadership potential, not a nurse already skilled in every possible nursing procedure. What I needed at the time was an internship for about six months in a hospital setting conducive to putting my learning into practice and giving me skills and confidence. I didn't even get an orientation let alone supervision or support.

The good part of the summer was working with a great group of nursing assistants and orderlies. My last day of work, they gave me a party in the medicine room and served donuts and lemonade. I ignored the rule about not eating with seculars and joined them inhaling the fresh donuts.

Later that summer, I received notification I had passed the state board exams. I made it! Yahoo! Even though I hadn't had much time to review, I placed fourth in my class of twenty-three. I needed that. After so long hearing Sister Robert Mary tell me how worthless I was, I had begun to believe her. But no more! The day I heard the news, I was so excited I wrote "R.N." on everything, even some toilet paper.

∽⌒ JOPLIN, MISSOURI ⌒∽

I felt I was in the big-time with my first real assignment, Saint John's Hospital in Joplin, Missouri. I would have preferred Denver where several of my buddies, Barb included, were assigned. At least one of my friends, Sister Mary Kent, was in Joplin teaching at the high school. She was a funny lady and I hoped I would be allowed to see her once in a while.

Being in Joplin was more of an adjustment than I thought it would be. There were only eleven of us Sisters: a superior of the house, a hospital administrator, a director of nursing, five floor supervisors, and three retired Sisters. Most communities had a few retired Sisters. Our three were sweet and would tell interesting stories about "life in the old days when things were really tough, dear."

My job in Joplin was to supervise a urology and orthopedics unit. The convent was tucked away on the far side of the same floor where I worked. It was a convenient arrangement but meant I didn't get much change of scenery all year. I was anxious about being a supervisor so fresh out of school with only six weeks of nursing experience under my belt. The Provincial Council wanted a Sister in charge of each floor, which was nice in theory.

But I knew nothing about supervising. I hoped I would learn quickly or at least learn to fake it. I had the feeling I wouldn't get much guidance, either.

The Sister who was the director of nursing oriented me for a total of two hours shortly after my arrival. She acted very strange and was anything but friendly. In a whirlwind fashion she pointed out things in the cupboards, rooms, and desks and then said, "It's all yours."

The floor had fifty-two beds which were usually occupied and was low on staff. The evening shift, for example, had one R.N. and three to four nursing assistants. I didn't know where to start so I got acquainted with several of the staff who were very willing to answer my questions when they had time. I tried to do some patient care each day to learn the routine. I couldn't supervise without knowing what I was supervising. I knew that much!

After two months I assessed my progress. The good news was I enjoyed nursing care. The bad news was my director of nursing didn't like me and let me know it. I couldn't seem to win no matter what I did. She had no love for four year BSN graduates and said we were "useless, totally useless." She, of course, was a three-year Diploma graduate as were the other Sisters who supervised a floor, which made their working relationships less antagonistic The director of nursing did all the hiring, firing, counseling, and staffing. She wouldn't discuss anything with any of the supervisors, let alone allow us to be a part of any management decision. The other Sisters seemed resigned to that arrangement but I had a hard time being discounted. I felt if I couldn't supervise, then I needed to be a staff nurse and get some good patient care experience.

We were to be available to our floors twenty-four hours a day, seven days a week. The director of nursing functioned that way.

In fact, when she heard an ambulance pulling into the emergency entrance in the middle of the night, she would be down there in minutes helping even if the nurses didn't need her. She acted upset with me for not waking up and helping my staff with accident victims admitted to my floor. Believe me I was so sound asleep I didn't hear the ambulances! I soon realized she enjoyed controlling us on the one hand and berating us for not doing our jobs on the other. She also insisted we do simple tasks like checking every single food tray for every single meal every single day. For this I went to school? The nursing staff on my floor had worked for her for so long they were used to the way she functioned. "Oh, that's just the way she is." I wondered if I was being unrealistic and would eventually adjust to her ways. I found out she had been a patient in a mental health facility the year before. That information helped me understand some of her behavior.

One person I did enjoy was my superior, the Sister in charge of the convent. She was new to Joplin, also, and was no match for the old-timers who were not about to pay attention to her. They kept doing things the way they had always done them. She and I tried to support each other, mostly by chatting when we could find the time.

My friend, Sister Mary Kent, would call every once in a while to cheer me up. She was full of energy and loved teaching high school. She managed to arrange a quick trip to Omaha for the two of us which just about saved my sanity. She needed a Sister companion to take a busload of her senior girls to visit the College of Saint Mary. Much to my amazement I was allowed to go. I called Mom and Dad to see if they would take six to eight girls in their home for the weekend. "They can sleep on the living room floor and won't be much trouble." "Of course, dear, we would love to have them."

The night of our arrival Mom, Dad, Marty, and the dog, Schotzy, were waiting in the living room when they heard a Greyhound bus roaring around the corner of their quiet neighborhood. "Hi, guys, uh, none of the other households came through so the rest of the girls will need to sleep in the bus parked in your driveway." Dad immediately realized that having the engine of a bus running all night would not go over so well with the neighbors. "No way," he said. "It's too cold out there." So, all forty-five girls marched into the Fangman house carrying blankets, pillows, curlers, hair driers, and overnight bags. They made themselves at home and started having a great time. Marty was more than happy to entertain girls her age.

Sister Mary Kent and I went into the house long enough to get the girls settled but we couldn't stay. For once, I was grateful for our regulations and we split as soon as possible to our nice, quiet convent. The next day we learned the details of what we had missed. Around midnight Mom found Dad sitting in his bathroom drinking a very strong scotch. That was the only place in the house he could hide from the noise and confusion. The girls took showers, washed their hair, and flushed toilets most of the night. My brother, Paul, came home in the wee hours of the morning to find bodies strewn all over his bedroom. He didn't say a word, just made a u-turn, and disappeared. The next morning my sleep-deprived parents made mountains of hot buttered toast and anything else they could find in the refrigerator. Sister Mary Kent gave the girls a lecture about being good visitors and they were much quieter the second night. When they returned to Joplin they sent a lovely lace tablecloth as a thank you for the hospitality and for having to clean up the mounds of dust bunnies left by so many bodies and blankets.

After about four months in Joplin, some confidence began to creep into my work. I hadn't realized how wobbly I was until my roots began to grow. However, I couldn't get rooted in the community of Sisters and felt like an outsider. I wondered if I was the one to blame. Could I fit into any community?

Since I was with the nursing staff day in and day out, I became friends with some of them. They seemed so much more human than the Sisters. They would look me in the eye when they talked to me, answer my questions without a cutting comment, and treat me with respect. I seldom got eye contact from other Sisters and when I asked them questions, I felt they minimized my concern. When I was alone in the privacy of the chapel, I allowed myself to cry. I prayed for strength and understanding. I was losing my ability to smile, to laugh, or to get excited about anything. I was becoming depressed.

I finally got to the point where I was willing to risk all the warnings we had been given in the Novitiate about leaving the convent. I was willing to give up family, friends, health, education, everything, to feel like myself again. More than once I visualized myself abandoned, without a job, crippled, and sitting on a street corner selling #2 yellow pencils. That thought gave me more peacefulness than when I imagined being a Sister of Mercy for the rest of my life. I didn't want to just endure my life; I wanted to enjoy and feel some contentment. I couldn't stop questioning everything I had been told. I didn't *want* to stop. The Catholic Church and the Sisters of Mercy had been such a big part of my life, but I no longer felt I could do what was expected of me.

I've often thought my dilemma in Joplin was similar to a woman in an abusive marriage. I was cut off from family and friends and had less and less confidence in myself. I doubted my own thoughts and kept vacillating between decisions.

One night I awoke from a deep sleep, sat up in bed, and realized I needed to leave. It was a very spiritual experience and I was shaken by the clarity of it. I felt no guilt or confusion. My recent prayers had been, "Dear God, since I cannot convince myself I should make a lifetime commitment to the religious life, please give me the grace and courage to leave."

The next couple of weeks were rough. Periods of doubt came back, of course. Eight years of conditioning were hard to overcome. I became increasingly frustrated at work with feelings of inadequacy, lack of control, and lack of respect from the director of nursing. I talked with my superior and she encouraged me to write a letter to the Provincial Council about my needs as a new graduate. They oversaw all the Sisters of Mercy in the Western Province. (There were nine provinces in the United States.) She herself was writing one to communicate her frustration. I hesitated putting my thoughts on paper. I feared they would think me out of line. But, after more praying and mulling, I decided I needed to speak up or give up. I labored over the exact wording and wrote the letter with every ounce of courage I had. I prayed they would receive it in the light I wrote it.

Two weeks dragged by with no response. The waiting was terrible; and, with the silence, I began to feel unimportant. I needed a response, any response. My stomach felt like it was in my throat and each day was an effort.

I clashed again with my director of nursing when she made some major changes on my floor without telling me. In desperation, I went to the Sister who was the administrator of the hospital. She said she had written a letter to Mother Provincial, also, but she didn't give me any details of the letter. I did not trust what she was saying but didn't know why. (I found out years later there was good reason for my being uncomfortable with her.

Several Sisters who had worked at the hospital in Joplin also wrote letters to Mother Provincial and did not hear back. Even though our mail was not censored, it did get put in the lobby office where the administrator could intercept any letter going to the Provincial House. Mine was most likely one of the letters not sent.)

In the meantime, Mom and Dad came to Joplin for a visit. They were having a nice vacation after Mom's discharge from an alcoholism treatment facility (which seemed to help for a few years). Without getting emotional, I admitted I was not happy. I didn't want to tell them everything but felt obligated to tell them something. I thought it would be a bit of a shock if I called them one day to say, "I'm coming back home!" On the other hand, I didn't want them worrying about me if I stayed. Dad's response was the usual: "We love you and want you to be happy."

I needed to talk to Barb! I wrote a long letter imagining we were chatting and walking up the hill back in the novitiate. I told her I was not planning on making final vows. I didn't mail the letter. Instead, I showed it to Sister Mary Kent who shook my conviction by reminding me of what we had been taught: no matter what I did in life, nothing could be more perfect than being a religious. I was so used to being told what was right for me that I began having doubts again. I felt so easily swayed! No guts. I could not believe how hard a final decision could be.

I respected Sister Mary Kent. The two of us decided I should talk with someone else. Mother Provincial? I felt I couldn't trust her after she didn't answer my letter. I was afraid she would either ask me to leave or extend my temporary vows for another year. It would have been easier if someone else made the decision for me but I didn't really want that. I knew I could not drag things on much longer.

Sister Mary Kent and I concluded I should talk with a priest.

I didn't know anyone in Joplin, so I approached my superior and she agreed to send me to Kansas City for a few days. Since the Ecumenical Movement, Kansas City had become a focal point of change within the Church in America. I was encouraged by articles in the Kansas City Catholic newspapers about the wonderful work some ex-seminarians were doing. The articles suggested that many were right in leaving the religious life because of the illogical and unreasonable facets of it. Before that, I'd read and heard nothing but derogatory remarks about "those who did not persevere." I thought someone in Kansas City would understand what I was thinking and feeling. I was allowed to go without a Sister companion. To top off all my confusion, my papers arrived asking if I wanted to make final vows. To hold off sending them back would be to admit my indecision. Without focusing, I signed and mailed them.

I talked with some of the Kansas City Sisters the first day and a priest the next day. I thought they would be more supportive of my struggle but they all said the same thing: I have the qualifications to be a good religious. Well, I knew that! They also felt most of my indecision arose from the particular situation in Joplin and the stress of working long hours. I could see their point. They recommended I stick it out for a few more months and things might calm down. If nothing else, I would get a break during the summer when I went back to Omaha with the rest of my band to prepare for final vows. As I listened to them talk, I thought I agreed with them. But I did not find peace in their recommendations. I knew my indecision ran deeper than they realized.

As I boarded the train back to Joplin, an older woman was getting off and we exchanged greetings. She handed me a book and said, "Here, dear, take this. I think you would enjoy reading it on your train ride." I did. I loved it. It was A *Ship Called HOPE* about a hospital ship that traveled around the world teaching and helping those who were in need. I hadn't known anything like that existed. What an opportunity that would be to work with an interesting, committed group of people. Could I be a part of that if I left the convent?

By the time the train pulled into the Joplin station, I felt I could have died from panic. Panic at the thought that my mind was still not settled after all I had tried to do. I needed to make a decision and stick with it! I needed to feel some peace of mind. To my knowledge, no one had ever voluntarily left right before final vows. The exodus from convents wouldn't start until a few years later.

When I arrived back at the convent, a letter from Mother Provincial awaited me. It said, "Since there is an indication on your report that you have had some questions about your vocation, I am asking that, before making your Perpetual Vows, you prepare a statement saying you sincerely desire to persevere in Religious Life." I had no idea who gave her that feedback. When I read the letter my heart chilled. An indication on my report! I was shocked and saddened that there was not one word of concern and no mention of my letter. All she seemed to want was reassurance I would follow company policy. So, to buy some more time, I sent a statement saying I desired to persevere in Religious Life. I didn't know what else to do. My conviction to leave had not held, but then neither had my decision to stay.

Barb called from Denver a few weeks later to find out if I had heard rumors going around that I had not been accepted for final vows. At first, her news shook me. Then, a tremendous peace calmed me. I began to pray I wouldn't be accepted but I received a letter of acceptance the very next day. The disappointment was almost physical. Plus, I had to pretend I was happy, with the news.

By June I was packing my trunk to go back to Omaha for the summer. I didn't know how to pack. Would I be coming back to Joplin? Would I ever again need all the stuff in my trunk? What would I be doing next year? I had agreed with the people in Kansas City who said I needed to get some rest, be with my friends, and get my perspective back. My fear was that I would be caught up in the excitement of everyone being together again and preparing for final vows.

The first weeks back, Barb and I spent hours talking and crying. She was vacillating even more than I was. One evening we became quite silly and plopped into a huge cart full of laundry, our legs hanging over the sides. We laughed about how uptight we had become. At least we hadn't lost our ability to giggle together.

On July 19, 1965, I FINALLY made the decision to leave, and I stuck with it! I don't know what ultimately convinced me but I just knew I couldn't make final vows. If I couldn't do that, I needed to leave. I told Sister Mary Cecilia, the Mistress of Juniors, who responded very kindly and arranged for me to talk with Mother Provincial that day. Waiting in the long, bare hallway to see her, I visualized closing my eyes, holding my nose, and jumping into water. No more thinking! No more vacillating! I heard birds singing outside the windows and felt they were singing for me.

When I was summoned into Mother Provincial's office, I was told to sit. I had no problem saying, "Yes, Mother, I've decided to leave." Her reply took me by surprise. "Sister, do you realize how much money we spent educating you?" They did spend a lot of money on me and I've always been grateful. But I didn't think that was the priority at the moment. I was expecting something like, "Sister, I'm sorry you've been so unhappy and I hope you will find peace. God bless you, dear." I sat there flabbergasted, not knowing what to say. My decision to leave was cemented by her coldness to me. That was the moment I knew I could make a clean break.

Barb also talked with Mother Provincial but would not talk to me about it. She had become more and more unsure and decided to renew her temporary vows for one more year. Her staying didn't affect my decision. I would've loved sharing the experience of leaving with her just as I had shared the experience of entering. But I wasn't about to try and talk her into anything. I was happy I was the one leaving. I knew it was the most difficult, soul-searching thing I would ever do in my life. I couldn't imagine making a harder decision. Eight years was a long time. But once the decision was made a tremendous peace came over me.

Mother Provincial wanted me out the next day so I wouldn't influence the other sisters. I could just hear the statement being said about me: "Sister Mary Janice has not persevered in her vocation." But I was thrilled! I did not have one minute of regret or confusion after that, only total relief. I had done my grieving already. I phoned Mom and Dad. They did not, in any way, indicate they were disappointed in me, and Dad repeated his earlier statements of, "We love you, Anne. Whatever makes you happy is fine with us. You are always welcome home." So much for all the dire warnings we'd been given about family rejecting us if we leave.

The next morning after breakfast one of the Provincial Council led me from the convent to the Provincial House where Mom and Dad had been instructed to come. The night before, I had informed some of the Sisters about my decision even though I wasn't supposed to tell anyone. They were happy for me because I was so happy. As I walked up The Hill, I looked back at some of my friends standing at the bottom of the steps watching me go. I smiled and clicked my heels in a gesture of pure joy. They laughed. I knew I would miss them.

Before changing out of the habit, I had to sign a letter:

July 20, 1965

Dear Mother General,

I hereby willingly, knowingly, and freely request permission to live outside the Institute of the Religious Sisters of Mercy from July 20, 1965 to August 16, 1965 when my Temporary Vows expire. After much prayer, thought, and consultation, I have decided that I do not have a vocation to the Religious Life.

I fully realize that I am bound by my vows of poverty, chastity and obedience and the service of the poor, sick and ignorant until August 16, 1965.

Therefore, in accordance with the above, I have made the following agreements with Mother Provincial:

I will remain outside the Institute without my religious habit from July 20 to August 16, 1965.

I will practice obedience by following the advice of my parents during this period.

I will practice poverty by not being extravagant in the use of money for luxuries, recreation, or personal wants.

I will guard my vow of chastity by refraining from anything that might endanger it.

I release the Religious Sisters of Mercy of the Union in the United States of America, Province of Omaha, from all obligations to me, financial and otherwise.

Signed,

Sister Mary Janice, RSM

(Anne Fangman)

It felt so strange taking the habit off, knowing I would never put it on again. I kissed each piece good-bye and laid it gently on a chair. The clothes Mom and Dad brought for me hung on my body. Mom had picked out the largest outfit she could find in Marty's closet not knowing my size. My feet felt like they didn't belong to me when I bent over and saw my white tennis shoes and my unfamiliar bare legs. I felt so peaceful, as if I were being let out of prison. I had been eight years struggling to convince myself I belonged, eight years trying to conform, and eight years of growing up. I felt eager to face whatever the rest of my life would bring. When I walked into the room where my parents were waiting, I was grinning from ear to ear. Dad hugged and hugged me. Mom cried. I never looked back. I can't say, "I leaped over the wall," but the change was just as dramatic.

HOME AGAIN

I don't believe the saying *you can't go home again*. Going home was wonderful! I felt lovely and loved. According to Marty, I didn't look very lovely as I walked into the house that first afternoon. "Pitiful, kid, pretty pitiful." She later admitted she had waited for me with some anxiety. She thought I would be stuffy and make her kneel down for prayers all the time. But I had no need to bring the convent home with me. I had had enough. "Man," she confided later, "what a relief it was when you acted like a normal person." I hardly knew Marty. She had evolved into a cool high school senior, or at least she kept telling me she was cool.

I was comfortable with myself so that everyone else relaxed and my first night out of the convent was fun. After the initial hours of sitting around gabbing with the folks and having dinner, Marty and I went through her closet to see which clothes would fit me. Her hearty laugh and her willingness to be my friend were so genuine. About 2:00 A.M. my brother Paul came home and cooked us bacon and eggs (his specialty). We shared his six-pack of beer and I became punchy enough to smoke my first cigarette since high school. Marty said I looked cute sitting at the kitchen table, wrapped in a blanket, smoking and drinking. She kept mumbling, "My sister, the Nun." It was such a treat to have fun and not feel guilty.

And did I ever sleep that night! After all those years of getting up at 5:00 or 6:00, I didn't budge until noon. It was so nice to hear the old greeting, "Did you sleep well, dear?" from Mom and Dad as I wandered into the living room. I became aware of so many things at once: soft towels, colored sheets, pretty pajamas, music, scented soap, and big mirrors. I talked endlessly. I had time to do what I wanted, when I wanted, with no bells to interrupt. I felt so peaceful. I couldn't imagine ever again giving up who I was as a person, becoming someone I didn't want to be, or living a life I didn't want to live.

My hair was a sight, all chopped and dull, but I didn't care. When I was in high school, the only hair tools we used were bobby pins, rubber bands, and barrettes, so I was all thumbs trying to use hair rollers. Marty nagged me until I made an appointment to get my hair trimmed by a professional. The hairstylist grimaced when he saw me.

"You want me to do something with this hair?"

"Yup."

"Who cut it!"

"I did."

"Looks like it. Why?"

"You don't want to know."

Marty also took on the job of making sure I knew the latest songs. The Rolling Stones' "(I Can't Get No) Satisfaction" cracked me up. I would burst into song and start dancing when it came on the radio. That song became my all-time favorite and I still turn up the volume when I hear it.

Every once in a while I would ponder how my life would have evolved had I not entered a convent. What kind of a person would I have become? Would I be as peaceful? Would I have gone into nursing and married soon after graduating? Sometimes I became sad, thinking I might have wasted eight years of prime time. Then I'd quote Popeye to myself, "I 'yam what I 'yam." Those eight years were such a part of me I could not comprehend me without them.

Going to the mandatory Catholic Mass on Sunday became a sporadic thing for me very quickly. Both Marty and I would skip Mass but didn't want Mom and Dad to know, so we'd get dressed, wave good-bye, and drive to a donut shop. Marty was so relieved. She had worried I would make her go to Mass "maybe every day!" Over coffee and donuts we added up how many times the average Catholic goes to church, totaled how many times I had gone to Mass in the convent, and came to the conclusion I was caught up to the year 2017! I decided that, in 52 years, when 2017 came around, I would consider going to church on a regular basis. I joked about going to church but I was very serious about needing distance from organized religion.

I was having fun driving a car alone, stopping for a cup of coffee, sitting and watching people. It was such a relief to be rid of the confusion, the vacillation, the guilt and the fear of those eight years. New feelings of contentment would warm me all over. I found myself walking down a street, grinning for no apparent reason. I enjoyed sitting while staring out the window, thinking of nothing in particular. I didn't need to rush, or jump at the sound of a bell, or try to force myself to think spiritual thoughts. My thoughts were spiritual; I just didn't recognize them as such when I first left the convent.

Getting a job right away helped with my adjustment. One of the sisters from a nearby Mercy School of Nursing hired me to teach. That helped me feel less rejected by "that old gang of mine." She ignored the flack from some of the more conservative sisters who believed ex-sisters were a bad influence and should be ostracized. I enjoyed the nursing students (none of whom were Sisters) and cracked up at their humor. They would make up names for fictional new students like Sharon Sharealike, Sam Hill, and Helen Back. Their messy dorm rooms with their life-sized posters of the Beatles were a far cry from the dorm rooms I had been used to seeing.

In addition to teaching all week, I worked on weekend nights at a hospital close to home. It was not easy staying awake, but I was so broke I needed to work as much as I could. I was amazed how much everything cost, especially since the color scheme was no longer black and white. I made a lovely mint green dress and enjoyed sewing on something soft and pretty. I looked good in mint green. Marty hated to shop but would tag along as my teen-in-the-know to prevent me from buying anything frumpy. What a treat it was to try on bras, slips and panties that made me look feminine instead of neutered. Mom, who was experiencing a few good years of sobriety, took me shopping to buy my nursing uniforms. I bravely went by myself to purchase gloves, coats, boots, and shoes and gleefully called everything MY, MINE, MINE, MINE.

Dad taught me how to write a check and balance a checkbook. Not only did my money have wings, it had jet engines! A good chunk of it I spent on a new car, which the whole family went along to help me find. At the dealership, I headed straight to a cute, red Chevy Nova Super Sport with bucket seats and stick shift. Dad teasingly said, "Anne don't you want this other nice, four-door, white car with automatic shift and regular seats?"

"Oh, Dad! That doesn't look like any fun."

For months I had periods of feeling out-of-it, like some Rip Van Winkle waking after eight years of being asleep. Parties were an effort. I, who was a chatterbox in the convent, would get shy at parties. Most people take their level of socializing for granted, but I had missed a few key experiences like flirting, dancing, dating and drinking. New situations confused me, and conversations frequently had me feeling lost. I didn't know the TV programs people were talking about. *The Avengers? The Fugitive? Bonanza?* Sometimes I regressed into old convent behaviors and would lower my eyes as if I still needed to keep custody of the eyes. Then I would struggle with myself to get out there and mingle!

I started dating a sweetheart of a guy who had a wonderful sense of humor and a sporty convertible. I felt safe around him, probably because he was very proper with me. I don't know how I would have responded had he put the moves on me. (Maybe regress into my wonder-what-the-Blessed-Virgin-would-do routine?) I was too scared to consider heavy petting, even though I thought he was very attractive, and I knew I didn't want to marry the first man I dated. I wanted to travel and experience something besides Nebraska and nursing and being a Nun.

I became zealous about getting my body into shape. Looking in a full-length mirror convinced me I was not exactly a perfect 36-26-36, so I joined a health spa that guaranteed to take inches off my thighs or money back. Two months later, they gave me my money back. All those years of praying hadn't done much for my muscle tone.

Over the winter I spent a good deal of energy mulling about what I wanted to do next. Since the school of nursing where I taught was closing in the summer, it was the perfect time to do something fun. I wrote to Project HOPE but was disappointed to find the ship had just sailed to Nicaragua for a year. A form letter said they would keep my application on file. It implied there were hundreds of applicants, and I was certain they were all more qualified than I was. Now what? One of my friends commented,

"If you want to travel so badly why don't you become an airline stewardess?" Who, me? Then I began to like the idea. I could travel and experience a touch of glamor, both definitely lacking in my life so far.

BRANIFF

Travel and glamor came my way quickly as soon as I worked up the courage to apply to some airlines. First I interviewed with United and was told that each airline was searching for a certain "look" in its stewardesses. I thought conservative United, with its navy and white uniforms, would like my fresh from the convent look. But, no, wild and crazy Braniff with colored airplanes and multicolored Pucci uniforms liked me and flew me to Dallas, Texas, for another interview. I had never flown before and hoped it wouldn't make me barf. I loved it! I felt as if I were in a fairytale flying above the clouds, watching the sunset, and circling over the lights of Dallas. Little ole Annie from Omaha was in the big time now.

The next day I wore a prissy yellow ruffled dress to the interview and realized, too late, that I looked like Miss Innocence compared to the other applicants in the waiting room. The interviewer was young and handsome and I had to control myself not to stare at his gorgeous blue eyes. In spite of Mother Stanislaus' warnings that ex-sisters would not get hired, I mentioned on the application about my years in the convent. I didn't think I should leave out eight years of my background. Mr. Blue Eyes seemed to enjoy asking me about those years.

"And how did you like being in a convent, Miss Fangman?"

"Oh, fine, thank you."

"Do you have plans for returning?"

"No, I've had quite enough."

"What did you like the most about the convent?"

"The food, I guess."

I didn't know what else to say! "Oh, I liked the discipline and wearing black wool clothes?" I thought my answers were on the dumb side, but he just laughed. He probably wanted to ask why I entered or why I left, but he didn't. People asked me these questions frequently, and I never knew quite what to say. It took me years to articulate the answers to myself, let alone strangers. I left the Braniff interview feeling discouraged, but a letter of acceptance arrived at home a couple of days later. I had barely made the age cut-off by getting into their July class. In 1966, airlines would not hire anyone over twenty-six and I would turn twenty-seven in August. The mandatory retirement age was thirty-two. I was just getting started and I was almost too old. Those were the days when even the passengers dressed up with men in suits, women in dresses, and children wearing their best outfits. The airlines wanted their stewardesses to look a step up from that, competing with the celebrities who were becoming the Jet Set.

I joined the training in Dallas with gusto, even though it meant going six weeks without a salary. Only board and room were provided. Forty-five sweet young things were in my class, and I was not surprised to find I was the oldest. As I listened to their conversations about dating and drinking I felt more like their mother than a peer. I had the feeling *I was the only twenty-seven-year-old virgin airline stewardess in the history of flying!*

Classes were a different kind of stress. All of a sudden I had to be serious about how I looked, how much I weighed, how

I walked, and how I talked. We certainly were not graded on our level of spiritual perfection. One student was dismissed for being overweight and that scared the rest of us; I was at the maximum 127 pounds for my 5'6" frame. Many of the students were using laxatives and vomiting to control weight, but that seemed a bit extreme for me. It was tempting, though. Instead, I watched every morsel that went into my mouth. I had lost my convent baby fat, but the body wanted to go back to 145 pounds. We would get weighed during class times, and we never knew when the moment of truth would come. We were quizzed every day and had to maintain an 85% average. This wasn't hard for me except for memorizing the names, titles, and pictures of fifty Braniff vice presidents so we could recognize them if they boarded our flights.

The Powers School of Modeling gave us a class on how to walk. The instructor, "Polly Powers," (our nickname for her) told me I walked like a duck. Going up and down stairs was a challenge for all of us since Polly expected us to do it without looking at our feet. I figured if I could do it in a habit, I certainly could do it in heels. Next, we tackled balancing food and drink trays. This was before the days of pushing a cart up the aisle so we had to learn how to bend our knees to keep our balance. Hitting an air pocket could be disastrous with stiff legs and a tray full of drinks.

The next step to physical perfection was a day at the beauty parlor for individual make-overs. They frosted, trimmed and rolled my hair and then gave me a three-hour make-up session. The instructor did one side of my face and I attempted to do the other. She had to do both of my false eyelashes. I couldn't quite master what felt like gluing a caterpillar on a moving target. I emerged from the salon to all kinds of attention. I had been transformed into a butterfly. People kept telling me I looked *just* like Julie Andrews. I had seen *The Sound of Music* and felt terribly flattered.

We had been told at our interviews we would have short hair because it went better under the uniform hats. But some of the girls cried during their hair cutting sessions. I was just grateful to have hair. In addition to putting on the make-up every day for class, we were mandated to wear girdles. I didn't mind the make-up, but a girdle made me grumpy, and I thought whoever invented them should have been shot at sunrise. We had fittings for our elegant and expensive Pucci uniforms. We were expected to pay half the cost (several hundred dollars) which would be deducted from our paychecks in monthly installments. We were starting to look like the advertisements for the Braniff Strip which showed stewardesses taking off layers of their bright, multicolored uniforms: suit and heels while greeting passengers, culottes (knee length shorts cut to resemble a skirt) and flat shoes while serving drinks, then dress and flats while serving dinner. Our uniform even had a coat, boots, gloves, and a space-age looking hat. Most of the stewardesses avoided wearing the clear plastic space helmet that went over the hat. It was a bit much but a wonderful change from the standard Salvation Army look of most airline uniforms.

〜

We were scheduled on observation flights so we could watch the senior stewardesses serve customers. These usually turned into working flights for us since the stewardesses insisted we help. So, I took orders, rushed back to the galley, mixed a tray of drinks, and ran back to serve them. Then I realized I had forgotten which drinks went where. The passengers, knowing I was in training, tried to be good sports. But they ran out of patience when I handed over a gin and soda or a bourbon and tonic.

"Miss, what did you put in this?"

"Um, what did you order?"

"This was *supposed* to be a bourbon and water."

"Be right back."

〜

Dating in the big-time world of pilots and stewardesses was a bit intimidating. My hesitant behavior around men was completely opposite from that of my roommate, Lori. She would come back from a date higher than a kite from drinking. Our class was housed in a motel while a new training center was being built and she would walk from room to room giggling and talking to everyone. She could have gotten kicked out for drinking but didn't seem to care. We had a class council which would meet over lunch and ground girls for coming in late or having men in their rooms. The training rules were so much easier than convent rules that I had no need to take risks, especially since they were only for six weeks.

I was becoming a guy-magnet but still didn't know how to be comfortable with it. I bought a bright pink bathing suit and bravely sat by the motel pool. I was very conscious of being in a bathing suit instead of covered head to foot by yards of black material and I felt all skin. It didn't help that Lori told the lifeguard I had been in a convent. He was very polite but full of difficult questions. I hadn't sorted out my own feelings so gave him some flip answers, forgetting how unusual it was to go from a convent to the airlines. Having lived the experience, it didn't seem unusual to me, but I didn't feel like baring my soul to just anybody.

Because the planes were available only at night, we had a week of all night emergency training. Dress was jeans and sweatshirts. We toured various aircraft stored in the hangars and practiced sliding down chutes and ropes. We had heard all the nicknames for the colored planes: super-carrot, the big pickle, blue bird of paradise, and used those names instead of their official names of 727s, Convairs, Electras, and DC7s. The instructors knew I was a nurse and would call on me for information about what to do if someone was hurt, but I think they were just trying to keep me awake as the night dragged into morning.

Toward the end of training we tackled all the paperwork, including how to bid a flight pattern for the coming month. The senior hostesses would get first pick, of course, and they were awarded the cream of the crop flights like layovers in Acapulco or short daytime flights. Many of them would arrange their monthly eighty-five hours of flight time around second jobs. Stewardesses were paid for time the engines were running so we rookies got the leftovers, the puddle-jumpers, which wasted hours at airports. I didn't mind. Any schedule was more exciting than what I'd done before.

I couldn't decide where I wanted to be based once training was over. The possibilities were Kansas City, which I thought was too close to Omaha; Minneapolis, which was too cold; or Dallas. I opted for Dallas where most of the interesting flights originated. Lori wanted Dallas, also, and asked me to continue being her roommate. Three other trainees had asked me to share an apartment with them, but Lori seemed much more interesting. So I thought, "Why not?"

She and I spent an entire weekend renting cabs to look at apartments, duplexes, and houses. The only place we liked was too expensive and too far from the airport to be practical. I became overwhelmed. It was the first time I had ever thought about all the details and expenses of having a place. I was used to someone else taking care of everything. After a long day of searching, I plopped on my bed and cried.

Lori and I finally found a furnished one bedroom apartment near the airport, thanks to her Sugar Daddy contributing part of the rent. She had arranged it without letting me know until it was a done deal. I had never met a Sugar Daddy before. He was a millionaire, very nice looking, and married. Lori was engaged to a guy back home in New Jersey but I didn't know about *him* until he phoned early one morning and woke us up. I couldn't begin to understand Lori but figured it was her life, not mine. The apartment was new, furnished, and lovely and I was excited to have a nice place.

Sugar Daddy helped us celebrate our new digs by taking us to an elegant dinner at the Old Warsaw, a classy restaurant in the Dallas area. We had champagne, escargot, filet mignon, and flaming crepe suzette. To top off the evening we went to a club and there the trumpeter sang *Happy Birthday* to me. Since Texas was a dry state at the time, we had to bring our own bottle or purchase a bottle at the club. It struck me as strange since it seemed to encourage more drinking instead of less. Also, there were states like Kansas that would not allow liquor to be served in planes flying over the state. I thought that was even stranger. The whole evening was the most luxurious time I had ever experienced. I *looked* luxurious in a yellow evening dress borrowed from one of the other students. Sugar Daddy had brought a dozen yellow roses when he came to pick us up, so I wore one in my hair. I was flying high with The Good Life.

⌐

Just as the six weeks of class ended, we received word we would have to wait at least a month before being assigned. This announcement brought a lot of moaning and groaning. Most of us had been told we would start flying immediately after training finished, but no go. I was ambivalent. I was broke and didn't know how I would go another month without a paycheck. But I was happy for the time to go back to Omaha, visit family and friends, and pick up my car. I was reasonably sure I would be based in Dallas.

We posed for class pictures in our lovely uniforms a couple of days before graduation. As I sat there waiting for all forty-five of us to get organized for the photo, I realized that my whole life was about uniforms: Catholic grade school and high school, convent, nursing, and now Braniff. Graduation day, Lori and I filled a cab with our few belongings and moved to our apartment. After oohing and aahing for a while, we rushed back to the dorm, changed into our uniforms and attended our elegant graduation dinner.

In the midst of that crazy last day, I received a nice, long letter from Patrick, my childhood crush. Just holding the letter sent emotion through me. Hearing from him about the last thing I expected. It was full of nice chatter about what he was doing. He was still with the Jesuits and studying to become an ordained priest. He sounded wonderful and I wondered if we would ever see each other again. The previous winter I had seen him when his mother invited me over during his visit to Omaha. If he ever left the Jesuits, I wanted to be one of the first to hear. We had known each other for so long and had followed such similar paths. There would be so much we would not have to explain to each other.

I didn't have much time for reflecting on Patrick as the whirlwind of graduation and saying good-byes took over. Braniff arranged for us to fly home on standby so I was up most of the night waiting in the airport for an available flight. About 3:00 A.M. I crashed on a plastic couch in the employee lounge for a couple of hours, and then had to rush to a boarding flight.

I arrived in Omaha sleepy and excited. Mom and Dad greeted me at the airport with compliments on my new look, but I could tell they didn't know what to make of all the changes. Once home I showed them how we did the Braniff Strip which must have given them doubts about the wisdom of my being a stewardess. I'm sure they had heard stories about "Coffee, Tea, or Me" and were inclined, like the rest of the public at that time, to believe they were true for all of us. I was impressed with most of the stewardesses I had met. They were a mature, well educated, and professional group. I sensed Mom and Dad felt I had rushed things after so many years of being sheltered. As far as I was concerned, I couldn't move fast enough. I did feel scared and overwhelmed, but I preferred those feelings to boredom. I was happy, so I knew my parents would be happy for me.

While in Omaha, I visited with dear, crazy Barb who had left the convent a few months before. She said she wished she had left when I did but now she was sure of her decision. She was back to the giggling, great-looking Barb I had known and I hated leaving her behind again.

I drove back to Dallas with a few items for the apartment taken from my parents' basement. I was broke, broke, broke and barely had enough to buy gas and pay for the new highway tolls. Mom and Dad would have been worried had they known, but they were struggling financially and I didn't want to ask them for money. There was no such thing as credit or debit cards then, especially for single women.

∽

The apartment felt empty. Lori was still in New Jersey. We didn't have a phone, so I used a neighbor's to check in with a supervisor at Braniff. She said there was still no word on when or where our class would be based. I was beginning to panic. It was the middle of September, and I needed to work.

Later that evening, I called home from a pay phone (collect, of course), and Dad said a letter from Project HOPE had arrived. I was afraid to ask him to open it. HOPE wanted me in Denver for an interview. Not now! I had just spent two days driving in the opposite direction. How could I possibly manage the time and the money to get there? I was not eligible for free passes with Braniff until I actually started working. I could hardly think straight. I thanked Dad and hung up. What did I *really* want to do? Would I ever forgive myself if I passed up an opportunity to go on HOPE? I thought I was finished with soul-searching for a while and here I was smack-dab in the middle of it again. I decided to take one step at a time. Just because they wanted me for an interview didn't mean they would hire me, right? I tried not to panic. Once again, I had no one around to talk to. I hated pacing and swearing alone. For someone who had been quietly stashed away in a convent, this was a lot happening at once. *Thank You God. Dang it!*

I tried not to think about HOPE for a few days. Instead, I

kicked into survival mode and got a part-time nursing job. The hospital was fine with my unpredictable schedule. They needed nurses so badly I probably could have worked the day of my interview if I had shown up in a uniform.

I came home from orientation at the hospital to Lori watching the telephone being installed. It felt so good having someone around. We unpacked boxes and trunks which made the apartment look like the remains of a cyclone. I had to borrow money from Lori who usually had plenty.

Our good-looking neighbor dropped over as we were cooking dinner; he had helped me unpack my car the day I arrived back in Dallas and had been hustling me ever since. He made me nervous. After dinner, Lori disappeared into the bedroom, and he started kissing me. One kiss was about all I could handle. I didn't want to be prudish, but I knew he was trying to get me into bed. He couldn't believe I was twenty-eight and a virgin. Just as he was making another pass at me, Lori walked back in the living room and casually informed him I'd been in a convent for eight years. His shocked expression made me wish I'd had a camera. I gotta hand it to him, he recovered enough to ask me out again.

᷍

About a week after hearing from Project HOPE, mulling over the pros and cons of driving verses flying to the interview, I took the financial plunge ($92.00) and flew to Denver. Dottie, the nurse who interviewed me, had been on several voyages, including the very first one to Indonesia, and was full of information about life on the ship. She was looking for nurses who were very flexible and she felt anyone who had convent, airlines, *and* nursing background was definitely flexible. She said she needed to go back to The HOPE office in Washington, D.C., before making an official offer but I could count on going on the Colombia, South America, voyage in February. I was stunned by the suddenness of her decision. I thought I had more time to not know. Dottie would be the director of nursing on the voyage and I knew right away I wanted to work for her. She was such a far cry from the Nun who had been my director of nursing in Joplin! Later, on the ship, she would tease me saying, "Here I was expecting this frumpy ex-Nun for an interview and in walks this glamorous woman with false eyelashes!"

There would be about fifty nurses on the ship. Since the nurses who had been on previous voyages got first crack at going again, twenty-five or so new positions would be filled from about a thousand applications. They wanted nurses with at least two years of teaching and/or administration experience. I'd had a year of each, although I certainly didn't feel the year in Joplin was very administrative and told her so. She didn't seem to care. Many applicants eliminated themselves by losing interest, getting married, or simply getting cold feet. Not this kid. I was too thrilled with the possibility of working in another country. I agreed to learn as much Spanish as possible because we would be doing everything in that language: charting, labeling, communicating with patients, and teaching local nurses. I became so enthusiastic about it I could hardly stand it! I had no idea the energy it was going to take adapting to Braniff *and* getting ready for HOPE. I had yet to know my limitations and felt I could do anything I wanted.

Before I flew back to Dallas, I went for a quick visit with my Joplin buddy, Sister Mary Kent, who had been transferred to Denver. She was her usual wonderful self and razzed me about my life of glamor. She never once indicated she was disappointed in me. Seeing her gave me an even stronger conviction that my decision to leave was perfect for me. She seemed content, and I was happy for her; I just no longer wanted to be like her.

I walked back into my Dallas apartment to find a telegram from Braniff requesting my presence at work in two days. The timing was perfect. Our whole class would be on reserve, which meant being on call in case someone called in sick or wound up with too many flying hours than was allowed by the FAA. My head started whirling with all the things I needed to get done. Just in time to stop me from going in circles, my amorous neighbor knocked on the door with another friend and a bottle of champagne in honor of my HOPE interview. I rustled up Lori, put on my dancing shoes, and the four of us went out for the evening. I had a grand time. Lori got blitzed and jumped into the apartment swimming pool fully dressed.

My first day of being a stewardess turned out pretty crazy. Early that morning I was awakened by a call to be ready for a flight in one hour. I could hardly remember who I was, let alone leap lickity-split into my Braniff body. I was throwing on my clothes and make-up when the hostess room called back to say, "Hang tight, we don't need you yet." I collapsed on the sofa. By the time they phoned hours later for another flight, my brain was functioning, and I was organized. I was nervous because I hadn't been watching what I was eating; but when they weighed me in the hostess room, I was a safe 124 pounds.

If we arrived in the hostess room with a dirty uniform, messy hair, chipped nails, or anything else that wasn't acceptable, we could be sent home without pay. I always passed inspection with flying colors, so to speak. At the time, I was glad they were so strict and I was proud to be part of a classy group. This was 1966, and the women's movement had just barely begun, so awareness of how sexist some of the rules were never entered my head. After the convent, this was a piece of cake! I felt so glamorous walking through the airport noticing people looking at me as if I were some sort of celebrity. It was a far cry from the curious stares I had received when I was covered in black.

My first flight was to Chicago with stops in Oklahoma City and Kansas City. Each leg of the flight was hectic because we served drinks *and* meals. It was a good thing the FAA wasn't watching; I wasn't exactly ready for landings. We were required, of course, to have all food trays put away, passenger seats and tray tables in an upright position, and aisles free of debris. Well, I tried. I was hauling trays back to the galley as fast as my legs would carry me. Much to my amazement I didn't spill anything that trip. I did, however, forget where we were landing and, in the middle of my announcement, had to ask a passenger.

My biggest problem over the next few weeks became sleep. I couldn't get any. I had already committed to working a few nights at the hospital. Then, when I tried to sleep during the day, the phone would ring with people looking for Lori. On a night flight to Denver, I realized I had caught a terrible cold and was near tears from an earache. The captain was grumpy and got mad at the stewardesses for not bringing him coffee. I mumbled something about the similarities between flight captains and physicians and brought him a cup. The following morning as we all stumbled to our hotel rooms hardly speaking to each other, I didn't feel very glamorous. I had heard many stories about stewardesses sleeping with pilots but never did pick up any clues of that actually happening except for Lori. I wondered if I were missing something. It wouldn't be the first time I was oblivious to what was going on around me.

Lori would breeze in and out of our apartment, usually on her way to a date with some man she had met on a flight. She would leave the place in a mess and I would clean up, unable to handle the chaos. Whenever she was around, she wanted to go shopping for apartment items. I hated spending my hard-earned money on bedspreads and wastebaskets, even though I knew we needed them. I got down to $0.46 in my checking account and $2.53 in my purse and had to borrow money from Lori again.

There were times I arrived home from a flight to find Lori and Sugar Daddy in the apartment. I was given no warnings of his comings and goings. Lori wouldn't consult me about much of anything and even had the apartment manager switch our twin beds to one double bed without asking or telling me. She was "tired of the inconvenience" of using a twin bed with all her boyfriends. Every time I tried to talk to her about our living arrangement, she would cut me off. I was still too polite to pursue an argument. I didn't know *how*.

One evening I came home to Lori and Sugar Daddy in the living room so I plopped on the sofa and started chatting. Next thing I knew they were kissing and rolling around on the floor. I heard Lori say something about my being there, and he whispered, "She doesn't know what we're doing, anyway." I looked straight at him and said, "The hell I don't!" We were barely civil to each other during dinner, and they at least had the decency to go to a motel afterward.

Several times I came home to Lori in the bedroom with some guy and I would have to sleep on the sofa. The next morning their rattling around would awaken me. I got tired of it very quickly. I decided that if Project HOPE didn't pan out, I would request a transfer to San Francisco where Braniff had begun Military Airlift Command flights to the Orient. On hindsight, that would have put me in San Francisco right in the middle of the "summer of love." I'm glad I didn't have to deal with that just yet!

My amorous neighbor stayed in the picture for a while longer. We had some fun dates going to a football game and to the state fair where we walked hand-in-hand, enjoying the lovely fall weather, sharing lemonade, and gawking like a couple of kids. It was easy to feel romantic around him, but I knew our relationship would end soon. He kept telling me, "I could fall in love with you and marry you if we didn't have such strong religious differences." Since we hadn't discussed religion, I had a hard time taking him seriously. He just assumed I was still very religious, which I wasn't! My thoughts about what I did believe hadn't become clear, but they were definitely changing.

The boring flights of hopping around Texas were interspersed with exciting trips. I had wanted a flight to New York and finally got called to deadhead (as a passenger) and work it back the next day. Lori was called to deadhead the same trip. We rode first class, sipping champagne, looking out at the beautiful clouds, and plotting our time in The Big City. Lori was jazzed about the opportunity to show me New York.

As soon as we arrived, Lori called Sugar Daddy who said he and his brother would take us out for a night on the town. We rode the subway to the hotel, changed, and walked around with me gawking at Times Square, Carnegie Hall, the Rockefeller Center, Central Park, Tiffany's, and the New York Hilton. Lori was a fun guide.

Back at the hotel, we gussied-up for the evening and met the guys for more champagne. Dinner was at Chez Vito, followed by the Top of the Sixes to view New York by night, and on to the Americana to see a floor show with Tony Martin. It was easy to fall in love with New York. We got back to my hotel room about 3:00 a.m. where Sugar Daddy's brother started kissing me and fondling my breasts. He had me flat on the bed before I had a chance to let him know I was not interested in sex. He was handsome, rich, nice... and married. He tried intimidating me, being nice, being pissed, everything. Finally, he sulked back to his hotel room. I didn't get the impression he was used to rejection. I stood in my room feeling very tired and very naïve. I also felt dumb, wondering if I may have led him on. I had just wanted to have a fun evening.

The following morning was awkward, to say the least. I dragged my body out of bed at 5:30 but the other three overslept while I paced in the lobby. I didn't know the guys' last name so couldn't call Sugar Daddy's room (where Lori was) or his brother's room. Just as I was about to hail a cab, they all showed up. We were supposed to report for flights an hour and a half before departure, but we *barely* made our flight after a frantic ride through the city in bad traffic. No one said a word in the car, and I was totally relieved when we finally pulled up at the airport. On the flight home Lori acted in a better mood and announced over the PA system that I had been in a convent. I couldn't help wonder if she was trying to get back at me for the night before. I never knew with her.

We made a brief stop in the hostess room to thank them for assigning us both to the New York trip and found out I had been awarded a flight pattern to Minneapolis for the coming month. I didn't really want to spend November going back and forth to Minneapolis. Nothing against the city, but I'd had my share of cold weather. Plus, I didn't want to spend a whole month visiting the same place when I was pretty sure I only had a few months left to fly. I said no thanks, I'll stay on reserve. I was tired of being on call but didn't want to miss the fun of different flights.

∽

Project HOPE sent a letter of confirmation the end of October. It was official: I would be going on the voyage to Colombia, South America, in February! I was thrilled. I was scared. I was overwhelmed. Lori and I celebrated by going shopping. She guided me to an exclusive dress shop that had no clothes racks. I had never heard of such a place. The sales ladies asked our needs and served us drinks while we tried on items they brought from a back room. The dressing rooms were huge and luxurious. I had no idea if I would have much use for a cocktail dress and a suit but I bought them anyway and had a wonderful time. I made the dangerous discovery that spending money could be good for the soul. It certainly beat making my own clothes!

Back at the apartment Lori and I broke open a bottle of champagne and toasted shopping, HOPE, us, Braniff, men, anything that came to mind. Then Lori vanished with one of her boyfriends. I was so wired I phoned everyone I knew to share the good news. HOPE had sent a very long list of things to get done: immunizations, passport, Seamen's papers, background reading, clothes, toilet articles, on and on. Once again I would be packing a trunk, only this one would be *much* more exciting.

I looked into classes from the Berlitz School of Languages and blanched at the price: $750 for one hundred Spanish lessons. Not only did I not have that kind of money, I didn't have the time to schedule a hundred lessons. What to do? I decided to live with a Spanish language book as my constant companion and study every free moment on takeoffs and landings, in between flights, and on layovers. One of the Braniff instructors gave me the name of a stewardess who would be willing to teach me Spanish for free. I jumped on that! She had lived in Colombia as a young girl and was able to give me fascinating background information about the country during our hit-and-miss sessions.

Things were not getting better with Lori. She complained about the noise *I* made while *she* was trying to sleep. I thought it was more the pot calling the kettle black. I was infinitely quieter and more thoughtful than she was, but that was just my *unbiased opinion*. She finally admitted she was grumpy because Sugar Daddy had called to tell her he didn't love her any more. Then he called a day later to say he still loved her but was going bankrupt and had taken his frustration out on her. In an attempt to smooth things over, I suggested we get gussied-up and go shopping. We once again became girlfriends over a delicious and expensive lunch at Neiman-Marcus. Then I watched her spend an absurd amount of money on a jacket for Sugar Daddy and a sexy nightgown for herself.

My less glamorous dating life was off and on when I could muster the time and energy. One of the first class passengers on a Chicago flight took another stewardess and me to the Playboy Club. It was exactly as I imagined: lots of flesh, money, beautiful people, and the undercurrent of sex. Then he took us to the Palmer House to see the comedy team of Alan and Rossi. I think the two of us enjoyed the evening more than he did. He turned out to be aloof and impersonal, almost weird. I was glad I wasn't alone with him. I wouldn't have felt safe.

I was never concerned for my safety when I was around the male flight crews. They were usually friendly and frequently we would go to movies or dinner once we arrived at our destination. The grapevine had passed on the information about my convent background so I would get grilled:

"What made you *enter*?"

"What was it like?"

"What made you leave?"

"You don't look the *type*!"

I was beginning to enjoy most of the discussions but still did not have much insight.

I didn't look like a composed, together ex-Nun on flights in and out of Denver, struggling to get food trays back in the galley before landing. On one particularly bumpy flight, I was balancing six trays in the galley when we hit an air pocket. I dropped every single one of them. *Nothing* missed me: butter, salad dressing, coffee, frosting, and even a little broccoli. My next cool move was to slip on the food and land on my derriere. All I could do was laugh. As the other stewardesses were helping me clean up, the plane hit another air pocket and we all landed on the floor giggling.

The one and only time the stewardesses were unkind to me was on a flight to Mexico. The scheduler from the hostess room had called on my day off to see if I could be ready in 30 minutes. She knew I wanted to practice my Spanish. I was almost sorry I went. The stewardesses in coach ignored me during the flight and then went off to the terminal in Mexico City without me. Earlier, I had told them I had never been to Mexico City and was eager to see the terminal, but they later said they "forgot." I sat in the bathroom on the plane and cried. On the flight back, the stewardesses in first class asked for my help. I think they had picked up on my frustration and were delightful to me. Some of the bilingual passengers went out of their way to teach me Spanish words and phrases, which helped pull me out of my funk.

I had been having a bad time for weeks, being hard on myself and not hearing people's compliments. My schedule of flying, working at the hospital, and getting ready for HOPE was taking its toll, and the things going wrong were looking worse than the things going right. The closer I got to the end of my Braniff days, the more I realized how much I would miss it.

During a period of trying to get my act together, I stayed

home to iron my uniform, soak in the tub, and do my nails. I started re-reading *A Ship Called HOPE* and couldn't put it down. It was past midnight before I finished the book, put on the last layer of nail polish, and turned out the light. Exactly one hour later the phone rang for a flight to Denver. In my stupor, I clobbered and smeared my semi-dry nails. All I could do was shrug and say, "Oh, well."

Hours later, as I was sitting and staring into space during a three-hour layover, I noticed I had cat hairs stuck on my nail polish, my uniform, my book, my tote bag, and my purse. A couple weeks before, Lori had brought her two HUGE black cats from New Jersey without warning me. They felt the same about me as I did about them: tolerance laced with hatred. If I did the slightest thing to upset one of them, like moving them so I could get into *my* side of the bed, Lori would get upset with *me*. They peed on my new wool winter coat, and even getting it dry cleaned didn't help the smell. As I sat at the airport looking at my hair-covered stuff, I fantasized about cat fricassee.

∽

December and January were spent being pulled in two different directions: enjoying everything about Braniff and getting ready to leave. The supervisors in the Hostess Room were so proud of my going on HOPE they did everything they could to help. They arranged a trip to Houston with a three-hour layover so I would have time to apply for my Seamen's papers. As I walked around the Houston shipyards, I felt incredibly self-conscious in my colorful Braniff uniform. At first I tried to ignore the dockworkers' whistles but finally bowed and curtsied. They clapped.

Later, I requested and got another trip to New York to do Christmas shopping. After arriving, I spent the afternoon walking around in a picture-perfect setting of softly falling snow, magnificent decorations, and lovely Christmas carols. On the flight back the passengers were in a holiday mood until, about ten minutes out of New York, the number three engine conked out. It made such a loud thud we were terrified until the pilots informed us we weren't going to crash. We headed back to New York, where the flight was canceled. That was fine with me! I spent the extra day sightseeing with the crew and going to the Broadway production of *Funny Girl*. The flight home was also hairy because of wet snow freezing on the wings during our stopover in D.C. I didn't relish the possibility of spending a night in an airport so close to Christmas, but it almost happened. We were the last plane to leave.

∽

I found being a stewardess to be fun most of the time, and I especially enjoyed sitting around between flights talking with other employees and picking up on the subtleties of working for Braniff. Stories circulated about goofy announcements stewardesses made on take-off and landing. At the time, Braniff was flying in and out of Love Field in Dallas and one stewardess announced, "Ladies and gentlemen, we are now loving in Land field." During a flight I was working, I was so distracted while making announcements, I said, "Ladies and gentlemen, for the convenience of the *patient* sitting behind you, please put your seats in an upright position." When the passengers deplaned, many of them limped or pretended an arm was in a sling.

I had worked a couple of trips to Acapulco and became enamored with my first walk on a beach and a resort town. I arranged a five-day vacation in Acapulco with another stewardess before quitting Braniff. We water-skied, ate at restaurants on the beach, gawked at the famous Acapulco cliff divers, and watched the sunset over the water. We met a couple of guys who took us dancing at Whisky-a-Go-Go and to a floor show at El Zorro. I discovered I liked Tequila, but it didn't like me. I got a bit goofy, tripped up some stairs, and landed very hard on my right knee. I felt no pain until the next day when the Tequila wore off. I limped around but wouldn't miss water-skiing that afternoon and deep-sea fishing the next morning. Carpe Diem! Seize the day! We even went to a bullfight, my first and (I swore) my last. Blood and gore is not my specialty. John Wayne was there, so I watched him instead of the bullfight. Ironically, our luggage was lost on the way home. I just laughed. I was in too good a mood to be upset. The trip had been wonderful and had cost me all of $50 because of the discounts given to stewardesses.

I hardly recognized the apartment when I returned. Lori had cleaned and left a note saying she was taking the cats back home. When she arrived that evening, she was too preoccupied with her own dramas to hear anything I had to say about my trip. It would be the last time I saw her but we didn't say much of a good-bye. I wouldn't miss her. The feeling was obviously mutual.

When my last week of flying finally came, Braniff informed me they couldn't give me a leave of absence because I had not been with the company long enough. I was disappointed. I had hoped to come back after the year with HOPE. Rehiring was not an option since I was already past the new-hire age. I worked my last flight with feelings of nostalgia. I would miss walking through the airport wearing my uniform and getting admiring looks, such a dramatic difference from the invisibility of the convent. Working with Braniff had helped catch up my emotional age to my chronological age. I no longer felt nor acted like an ex-Nun, even though I still had many more adjustments to make.

My awareness of those adjustments was minimal since I was too busy having fun. Actual adjustments would come over the years as I lived my life. But, so far, I had proven to myself I could handle a life of glamor. Now I looked forward to a challenging professional experience and learning the customs and culture of a new country.

CARTAGENA, COLOMBIA

I was a minor celebrity for the few weeks back in Omaha before leaving for HOPE. Braniff had arranged a feature article in the local newspaper and some fun interviews on TV. The interviewers were more interested in my convent experience than my going on HOPE. The ship, they could understand; the convent, they couldn't begin to comprehend.

"How long did it take you to adjust to being out of the convent?"

"Oh, about a day."

It was a flip answer, but as honest as I could be at the time. I had been so happy to be out of the convent, I adapted quickly to the comfort of being home. I didn't need to think about all the things I had missed and all the experiences I hadn't had. I would become aware of them much later as I began to realize what had been missing in my emotional development.

Before I could say "Presto! **Chango!**" it was February, and I was in Philadelphia walking toward the ship. The hundreds of people waiting to tour The HOPE blocked my access so I set down my *very* heavy luggage and stared at the ship. She was beautiful sitting in the harbor all newly painted white. The sight of her thrilled me. I stood there grinning. A policeman saw me and asked if I needed help getting on the ship. Was it the goofy smile or the huge suitcases at my feet that clued him in? He did a Moses act and parted the crowd so we could get through. People were staring at us.

I was greeted with a warm welcome aboard ship. One of the "old Hopies" took me to my room/cabin. I would be sharing it with three other Hopies who had already arrived and were unpacking. One was a nurse, one a pharmacist, and the other a nutritionist. Being a rookie I got a top bunk. Even though ours was one of the larger cabins, we didn't have much elbow room. But we did have the luxury of a small sofa that served mainly as a place to throw junk. My trunk was waiting for me, so I spent the next few hours unpacking and chatting with my roommates. We were pretty puzzled about where to put things since we each had two small drawers and half of a very small closet. Drab green paint covered walls, ceilings and floors so we made plans to buy pink flowered Contact paper and pink rugs and pillows. Each of the corridors had acquired a nickname during previous voyages. Mine was called Convent Corner, of all things. I was told the name came from the group of non-partying nurses that had lived there on a previous voyage. As far as I knew, there had not been ex-Nuns as staff on the ship.

Navigating around the ship was hard on my shins. The doors had about a six-inch frame at the bottom that I tended to trip over instead of step over. I wandered from room to room chatting with nurses. One dryly commented her room was so small the steward would think it was a closet and never make the bed (one of our few perks, a room steward!). I peeked around the corner and agreed. There were no bathtubs on the ship and the shower stalls were very small. Almost every time I used one, I would bump my elbows, drop the soap, and struggle to reach for it. I usually tripped getting in and out because the showers also had frames on the bottom. I kept telling myself I was trainable.

The first morning we were told to report promptly at 9:30 for a fire drill, which meant hurry up and wait in our life jackets in the cold. We needed those fire drills. The HOPE was a World War II Navy hospital ship, the Consolation, brought out of mothballs and, through President Eisenhower's influence, sold to Project HOPE for $1.00. I didn't want to know how rickety she was. To entertain ourselves while waiting for the fire drill to proceed, we harassed the late arriving staff as they struggled up the steep, snow-covered gangway.

There was an elegant cocktail reception at the home of a HOPE physician that evening. I managed to connect with a darling guy who was helping prepare the ship for sailing. We danced and talked. It was all so romantic, and I spent the night with him in a motel. I could say it was my "first time," but we didn't do anything more than kiss. I still wasn't ready to be swept off my feet so I gave him the clinging-to-the-bedpost-I'm-not-that-kind-of-a-girl-I've-never-done-this-before speech. Poor guy, he was so patient with me. I was not ready to have sex with someone I had just met, even though I had been no good at letting him know earlier. Besides that, I couldn't imagine finding out I was pregnant part way through the voyage. It was one of those situations where I knew I had a lot to learn.

The next morning we woke up to a blizzard and had a terrible time getting back to the ship. I panicked. I thought we were going to miss the sailing. It turned out everyone else had just as much trouble and our departure was delayed several hours. He and I roamed around the ship chatting and enjoying each others' company. I hated to say good-bye. We corresponded several times that year, but never pursued our relationship any farther. He might have been one of the good ones I let get away.

Departing ceremonies with the Colombian ambassador, the mayor of Philadelphia, and other assorted important people had to be canceled. It was snowing so hard that only a handful of people persevered long enough to see the ship leave. We waved and threw some token confetti. It felt anticlimactic. I'd had visions of a grand departure with massive amounts of streamers, music and fanfare, just like in the movies. Instead, we spent the last few minutes in Philadelphia tying down hospital equipment so things wouldn't go flying all over the place when we hit rough weather. That evening, the staff got a warm welcome speech from the founder and president of Project HOPE, Dr. Walsh, as we were assembled in the lecture room. He was a very charismatic man and totally devoted to HOPE. The staff had nicknamed him Big Daddy.

It felt wonderful to be on our way. One of my roommates, Mel, had been on the ship in Peru, so I picked her brain about what it was *really* like. She made everything seem so much more real. According to the book I had read, HOPE stands for Health Opportunity for People Everywhere. The first voyage was in 1960 to Indonesia and South Vietnam, stopping about a month in each port. After that first year the time was extended to ten months in one port city so the staff could work more closely with the universities and schools of medicine, nursing, pharmacology, dentistry and so on. Other voyages had been to Peru, Ecuador, Guinea and Nicaragua, making ours the sixth voyage. The ship came by invitation from the host country with their full support in providing personnel to be trained. They also paid part of the expenses. Our main purpose was one-on-one teaching while providing patient care. Each of us, including the staff in housekeeping, supplies, and so forth, would be assigned a local counterpart while on duty.

The ship was noisy and crowded. She wasn't a luxury liner. She was good-sized, though, 530 feet long by 71½ feet wide. The very lowest level of the ship was the hold, where supplies and our trunks were stored; above that was the engine room; then came the lower deck, which held pharmacy, surgery, intensive care, x-ray, physical therapy, a lecture room, and a few offices. The next level up was the main deck, which had the rest of the patient care areas: female wards, male wards, and pediatric wards, along with the administrative offices. The next two levels—the promenade deck and boat deck—were staff quarters; the top two levels were the sun deck and the helicopter deck. Grace Lines, based out of New York, provided the ship's crews. Several of the officers had been on more than one HOPE voyage.

The first night at sea the ship rolled and pitched so much I was actually glad for the cumbersome side rails on my narrow top bunk. The snow on the decks started melting as we headed south along the coast, leaving the colored streamers of our feeble departure festivities. On the third morning the sea became calm, allowing me to wander outside to smell the air and enjoy a few snatches of sun.

We kept busy cleaning the hospital areas, which had plenty of dirt from being in dry dock for repairs. My assignment for the year was 4C, the mens' ward, where I helped put Spanish labels on supplies, charts, books, and doors. It wasn't easy thinking in Spanish so I was grateful for the nurses who were fluent from being on previous voyages. When the ship was used by the Navy, it had two rows of beds attached to poles. Since we would be taking only about 100 patients on board for teaching cases, the top row of beds had been removed.

A Catholic priest and a Protestant minister rotated onto the ship for two months at a time like the physicians did. It would be noticeable if I didn't attend the one and only Sunday Mass available and I struggled with being obvious about my "fallen" status. It didn't help that Big Daddy himself was Catholic and attended Mass faithfully. Word had spread about my having been in the convent, so there was no way I could deny being Catholic. Sometimes I went, sometimes I didn't, and it wasn't long before I didn't go at all. Looking back, it seems it was relatively easy for me to abandon a ritual that had been such an important part of my life for so long. Mass was part of the larger picture of being in the convent and I felt the need to shed as much of that experience as I could.

The days at sea flew by with all the projects we needed to accomplish. We had an orientation session with Dottie, our director of nursing. My first impression of her was accurate—she had a great management style. She said each one of us was hired because we were competent, and she trusted that we would do a good job. "So let's get going on your first assignment which is taking boxes out of storage and figuring out where everything goes!" We muttered about being under-challenged but we were glad to do anything she asked. The assistant director (nicknamed Ass Director) would come around the wards after we cleaned to see if we passed "inspection." I accused her of being trained by Mother Stanislaus since she made us re-do the cleaning more than once. Scrubbing floors was my specialty, at least when I could keep track of my bucket. I would turn around to get more water and discover the bucket had slid to the other end of the room. I was glad I had my sea legs so I could maintain balance while retrieving the thing.

In the evenings I wandered around the living quarters meeting staff. I was in awe of people's diverse backgrounds and interesting personalities. It was so nice not having a bell ring for night silence stopping our conversations mid-sentence! I could stay up as long as I wanted, talking to whomever I wanted, and not be accused of having a Particular Friendship. Life was good. One evening we watched a documentary about HOPE which had won an Academy Award. It made me proud to be a part of the Hospital Ship HOPE.

Several days later we stopped in Miami for two days of publicity and fund raising. Boats and helicopters escorted us into the harbor and Navy jets saluted. Hundreds of people lined up waiting to tour the ship. We wore sparkling clean uniforms and became part of the impressive picture of HOPE, the big, white medical ship out to help the world. The thrill of it all was tempered by aching feet as we stood for the endless speeches by the mayor, the governor, representatives of this, and chairmen of that. Then Dr. Walsh, with his flair for the dramatic, kissed each one of us nurses as we started down the gangway. The crowd loved it. My roommates and I stayed on shore long enough to do some last minute shopping and then rushed back to help with tour groups. A lovely reception on the helicopter deck was held for all the big donors. I wore the expensive cocktail dress Lori had encouraged me to buy in Dallas and was grateful for her influence. I looked great. I felt great.

The next morning there was a line at least three blocks long of people waiting to tour the ship. The family of one of the pilots I dated at Braniff managed to find me. I was surprised! He had kept me at arm's length and never said a word about his feelings. According to his family, he had talked about me several times. I wondered if I had missed something about the relationship.

A local physician had put a notice on the ship's bulletin board to call if anyone needed a ride, so I called. Several of us wanted to go to the beach. His wife picked us up in their plush Rolls Royce and drove us to their boat which took us to a secluded cove. We were having such a grand time that we didn't head back until the last minute. The traffic near the ship was so jammed we almost missed the 8:00 P.M. departure (was this becoming a pattern?). As the ship pulled out of the harbor, cars were lined bumper-to-bumper honking their horns good-by. Then, as we passed the high-rise apartments, people in the rooms blinked their lights off and on. It was all very emotional.

The following morning we had another fire drill. Only this time we didn't take it seriously. We had been instructed to show up with long-sleeved shirts, long pants, and other items for protection if adrift at sea. Some of us smart alecks showed up with high-heeled shoes, slinky gowns, cigarette holders, stereo equipment, lounge chairs, make-up cases, and liquor. The officers tried to ignore us.

We sailed past Cuba and Haiti. The nights became balmy with lots of stars so I spent my evenings walking on deck and soaking in the wonderful smells and sounds of the water. It felt so good to be at peace with myself and know my spiritual life belonged to me.

One thing I learned early about Hopies was they liked to drink and talk. Most of us were in our late twenties to, probably, fifties, a mix of male and female, and we still had the energy to party. Happy Hour every afternoon before dinner was a time for us to relax and blow off steam. Rule number one: no Spanish, only

English. The liquor was duty-free so drinks were only a quarter. Sometimes I would play bartender, which gave me a chance to chat with even more people. We would continue conversations at dinner in our cafeteria-style dining room where the food was good and the ambiance was marginal.

~

The HOPE arrived in Cartagena on February 16, 1967, all clean, organized, and ready to save the world... or at least this part of it. The ship circled around the harbor, killing time before the inevitable welcoming ceremonies. Later, during the reception on the helicopter deck, I struggled with the rapid-fire Spanish. But once I got a clue about what was being said, I would jump right in. Then I would get lost again and resort to sign language. I learned to say, *mas despacio, por favor*, meaning, "please, go slower." After the reception, several of us migrated for more partying in the second mate's cabin with a few Colombian doctors. One of the Colombians kept invoking "Bill Shakespeare" to help him with his English. He proposed marriage to me... or something obscene. I wasn't sure which.

The next day we toured Cartagena. It is a beautiful city with the old part, El Centro, surrounded by a fortress-like wall. It had not yet established its current drug-related identity. I saw my first open-air marketplace with meat covered with flies. It didn't take me long to realize the Colombians didn't have the luxury of cellophane wrap, refrigeration, or a lot of other things I took for granted.

The local charity hospital, Santa Clara, had been converted from an old monastery. The wards surrounded a big courtyard, where patients wandered around looking for the rare places to sit. Next we visited the maternity hospital where wards held *two women to a bed.* The patients had to walk through the delivery room to get to the bathroom, even as a delivery was happening. I was stunned to see the physician who was delivering a baby casually smoking a cigar. What really shook me, though, was the placenta thrown on the porch where the vultures ate it. I kept telling myself that it was an efficient system of disposal. My nursing experience had been so provincial that I knew I had a lot of adapting to do.

That evening we went to the Palace of the Inquisition for a cocktail reception. I tried not to think of the history of darkness, torture, cells and chains, but the place fit the name perfectly: high walls, long dark halls, huge trees, and an aura of intrigue. As we entered the courtyard, an orchestra began to play as if we were royalty. I quit feeling royal, though, when I noticed blocks of ice on the dirt floor being chipped for our drinks. The Colombians were proud of themselves for even having ice. According to them, we North Americans needed our hot drinks too hot and our cold drinks too cold, but they wanted to please us. After the reception, several of us Hopies headed to the Americana Hotel for dancing and I learned some wild South American dance steps from very willing local men. The music was a mixture of Latin beats and songs from the United States. When they played a familiar song, Dr. Walsh was out on the dance floor doing the twist. I knew then I was with people I could enjoy. Typical of us Hopies, we came and went crammed in the back of a truck, nice clothes be damned.

My roommate, Mel, and I overslept the next morning. Our Ass Director had to come into our cabin and shake us awake. I mumbled something about slave labor, threw on clothes, and grabbed coffee. Some of us felt incapable of organizing medical supplies, so we kept busy with the mindless task of punching holes in paper for notebooks.

Mel and I got our second wind in time to go to another party that evening at a ranch outside of town. It was hot and noisy and several older men kept flirting with me. I tried to be polite, knowing I represented HOPE. Colombians love to party all night, but we insisted on leaving while we were still coherent. The next day the backs of my legs drove me crazy with itching. The woven chairs at the party had been full of gnats and my short dress hadn't done much to protect me. I was miserable until I got my hands on some Benadryl!

Life on board ship became routine very quickly. The memory of Mother Stanislaus would periodically haunt me, and I would be compelled to tidy the cabin. I was the only one of the four of us who had that compulsion, however. There was so much stuff on our tiny couch we couldn't sit on it. I finally realized I was fighting a losing battle and gave up my quest for tidy. I seemed to have an ability to attract messy roommates.

Work began in earnest when our physicians went to Santa Clara Hospital to meet with the local doctors to choose patients for the Ship. The nurses' schedules would rotate one week of nights, one week of evenings, and then a week or more of days. We would get our bodies adjusted to one shift and then switch to another. But if we had stayed on evenings or nights, we would have missed a lot of the fun so we put up with the crazy schedule. It was a good thing most of us were young.

I wasn't too happy being on nights right off the bat. I was the least fluent in Spanish of any of the nurses, and I didn't have a local counterpart yet to help me communicate with patients. The first night was awful. One of the patients kept moaning. And I mean *moaning*. I couldn't figure out his problem and was convinced he was in severe pain. When I realized all he wanted was a glass of water, I wanted to dump one on his noisy head.

Part of being on nights was learning to drink some of the

worst coffee in the world. One of the officers thought he was doing the night nurses a favor by making coffee and bringing it to us every couple of hours. I swore it must have been in the coffee urn for several days. Either that or he forgot to rinse out the urn cleaner before making a new batch. I tried to be grateful. It was hard to think we were in the land of Juan Valdez (who was made famous in coffee commercials on American TV at the time).

I adjusted (and I use that term loosely) to being on nights, partly because I was too busy to think about anything but getting the job done. Mel was on nights in intensive care, so we would meet for breaks. She was encouraging, telling me I would eventually learn Spanish. I had my doubts in the mornings as I struggled with giving the shift report to a batch of bright-eyed local nurses and a couple of HOPE nurses. I was so punchy from lack of sleep, I could hardly think of what to say in English let alone in Spanish, and usually stopped partway through sentences to look up words in the Spanish dictionary. After report, I would hurry to bed thinking I was going to crash for several hours. All of a sudden I would be wide-awake. Too much coffee. I would toss and turn until dinner time and finally get up for something to eat.

One of the hard things about being on nights was that everyone else was heading for bed as we were heading down the stairs to work. A big perk, though, was the four days off that followed. As we dragged through the long nights, Mel and I met with the other night nurses to plan how we wanted to use our wonderful four days. We decided on a trip to Bogotá, the capitol of Colombia, high in the mountains at 8,700 feet.

"I want to eat where there are small tables and we get served."

"I want to sleep in a real bed."

"I want to soak in a bathtub!"

After our last night, we grabbed a few hours of sleep and

then caught an Avianca flight. We had been strongly advised not to go anywhere by car since we gringas would be prime targets for banditos. We didn't argue. We were also advised to protect purses and watches since Bogotá was considered the pickpocket capitol of the world.

Bogotá was beautiful. With its mountains and cool air, it looked and felt completely different from the coastal city of Cartagena. Prices amazed me. A delicious steak dinner cost $2.00 (American dollars). The four of us gleefully shopped for presents for the folks back home. I bought two beautiful wool plaid *ruanas* that were the local version of the poncho.

As we headed back to the airport I realized I could actually understand what the cab driver was saying because the Spanish spoken in Bogotá is Castilian and much crisper than the guttural version spoken in Cartagena. Learning Spanish in Cartagena was like learning English in Brooklyn. No wonder people in Bogota had trouble understanding us!

Once back on the ship I worked evenings. My two young counterparts were Columbian *auxiliaries* which are very similar to nursing assistants. They were nervous about being on the ship, and I was nervous about being unable to communicate. They had minimal medical education or experience, so they weren't much help with patient care in the beginning. After a couple of evenings I planned to cover the concept of equipment sterilization. I dropped that idea after trying to explain how to take a temperature, pulse, and respiration rate. We managed to get the work done but I had to stay late to do the charting *in Spanish*.

We Hopies had long periods of plain, hard work along with hours of plain, hard boredom. But then we had some inspiring moments. One of them came from a Canadian destroyer that had stopped in Cartagena. The crew toured The HOPE and then gave us a party on their ship. Later that night, as they sailed out of the harbor, they signaled a message to us: "And now abideth Faith, Hope, and Charity, these three. But the greatest of these is The HOPE."

We also had visitors from a U.S. cruise ship that arranged a fund-raising tour of The HOPE. Once again we would be tour guides. One of the visitors from the cruise line was so impressed with our work he donated $50,000 on the spot. Later, the other visitors took up a collection for another $50,000. I couldn't comprehend having that kind of money, let alone being able to give it away. Dr. Walsh told us some of the visitors were crying because they had not realized Americans were doing this sort of work and they expressed feelings of inadequacy because all they had to give was money. I was beginning to feel a deeper appreciation for how privileged I was to serve on The HOPE. Broke, but privileged. That evening the visitors gave a big party for us. Their ship was so luxurious it made the Ship HOPE look like a poor cousin. But we were treated like royalty. We talked, drank, and danced to lovely orchestra music till the warning whistle blew for their departure at 2:00 A.M.

After-party gab sessions evolved back on The HOPE, of course. Hopies were great at sitting around philosophizing and I learned a tremendous amount participating. That night our discussion included religions. Are all religions the same? What makes one religion different from another? I had been raised to accept that baptism in the Catholic Church and belief in Jesus Christ were essential for salvation. I was hearing for the first time what other religions believed just as adamantly. It was finally dawning on me that the Catholic Church was just one of many churches, not necessarily the one and only church. Of course during those discussions, we had to include the topic of sex. How much do you need to care about someone before having sex? What does it mean to have sex? I heard the pros and cons of the "wait for the one right person before sex" theory and realized I did not feel as rigid about the subject as I had before. It hadn't occurred to me till then how the role of women had been defined to dominate us, especially in the Catholic Church.

Periodically, we tackled the subject of democracy. What made us think the American way was the only way of doing things? Democracy is wonderful but is Democracy the only answer? A light bulb went on and I realized Americans are not always right. Often we act as if we have all the answers. The recently popular book, *The Ugly American*, was not fiction. It was reality. I began to question just about everything I had learned up to that point in my life and felt a gradual, and sometimes not-so-gradual, shift in my belief system. The shift felt liberating, and I was amazed at how open I was to new ideas after so many years of hearing that one way was the only way.

Having my eyes opened in many areas became a way of life for me. It had never crossed my mind that a person might not know how to use a shower. One afternoon, I was admitting a patient to the ward and gave him a pair of pajamas, a towel and washcloth, and pointed him to the showers. He obediently headed to the shower clothed and dirty. Twenty minutes later, he came out of the shower area clothed and dirty... and dry. I realized he had no idea what I had asked him to do. I proceeded to demonstrate how to turn on the shower and explain what to do with the pajamas. I was perfecting the fine art of sign language.

Many patients found pajamas a source of wonder since most of them did not have such things and were used to sleeping in their clothes. More than once I had to explain about sleeping between the sheets or patients would spend the night on top of both sheets.

Other situations demanded stronger responses. In desperation, I perfected how to say in Spanish, "No spitting on the floor!" after getting grossed out by slipping and sliding on the stuff. I would hand each patient a paper cup and explain, in a tone of voice that left no room for doubt, the need to use it. They complied.

The first patient death was hard to take. He had been on the ship for diagnosis and treatment of a tumor and many of us had become fond of him. His death was sudden, and we were concerned the locals would interpret it as an indication of our incompetence. We didn't want the Colombians to be any more skittish about coming on the ship than they were already. Everything was so new to them: the bigness of the ship, the air conditioning, the strange-speaking Americans, and the cleanliness of the wards. All we could do was explain why the patient died and keep on going as best we could. We showed a different side of ourselves then, one of knowing our limitations.

Meanwhile, we worked on our patience with ourselves. Dr. Walsh gave us pep talks and encouraged us to maintain a sense of humor. Once the staff was relatively settled, he went back to the States for more fund raising and planning future voyages. The night before he left, we dressed up for a champagne dinner by candlelight in our less-than-romantic dining room. One of the guys couldn't quite manage the whole look and showed up in a tuxedo jacket with Bermuda shorts. During the rest of the year, we dressed up once a month to remind ourselves that we could still be civilized and dress for dinner in something other than cut-offs, flip-flops, shifts, or uniforms. Instead of going through the cafeteria line for these special dinners, the Rotators (physicians) would serve us. We loved being waited on and would mimic the local custom of calling "Yoo-hoo, waiter!" at intervals during the meal.

Living on a ship in a foreign port kept us pretty much out of touch with current events in the States. Every so often a *Newsweek or U.S. News* and *World Report* would appear in one of the lounges and we would scan it for major events. Movies were also scarce. Once a month a movie would be flown to the ship and shown on the sundeck after dark. The first one we saw was Hard Day's Night, and watching the Beatles cavort around was just the dose of silliness we needed. Before our monthly movies we would crowd around the huge stove in the ship's galley vigorously shaking foil-wrapped containers of popcorn. Then we would grab our deck chairs and maneuver for good spots like a bunch of kids at a Disney film. Someone invariably started throwing popcorn and yelling, "Popcorn fight!" Years later, I would describe HOPE as a water-based M*A*S*H unit. There were many similarities.

It didn't take long for the honeymoon phase of being on The HOPE to be over and the realities of life on the ship to set in. Old Hopies said it was normal to have an emotional slump every few months. We were doing difficult work. I found myself being irritable with the constant ship noise and all the people. It became harder to sleep during the day when I worked nights or evenings. With four of us in the cabin, one of us was always trying to get ready for work or catch some sleep, and the poor steward never knew when to make our beds.

At a time when my slump was at an all-time low, we heard about a Colombian mail strike with rumors that excess mail was being dumped in the ocean. I had no way of knowing if this was true, but the idea of my precious mail floating somewhere in the ocean made me want to cry. I began to get lonesome for my family and *Omaha*, of all things. I called home with the help of the ship's dispatch, but we could barely carry on a conversation because of static and having to say, "Over," at the end of each sentence. About all I accomplished was telling Mom and Dad I loved them and missed them. Then I got a letter from Crazy Barb saying she was getting married! Our lives were going in such separate directions and I missed her. I had to accept we probably never would be as close as we once were and that made me feel even more lonesome.

To help ease my slump, one of the Hopies invited me to stay overnight at a local friend's beach house. It was just what I needed. It was so peaceful and quiet! I sat outside watching the sunset and then dozed in a hammock listening to a Miles Davis jazz album playing inside the house. To this day I can remember the contentment of falling asleep to the sound of the waves gently hitting the shore.

Work finally took on a routine and my Spanish improved. My boss, Dottie, sat in on a morning report and said she was very impressed with how well I was communicating. Did that ever help my morale! Then a few days later, during a team conference with my Colombian students, I realized they were following what I was saying. I stopped and said (in Spanish, of course), "You understand me!" They laughed and clapped. They had been struggling with my Spanish as much as I had.

I also learned to appreciate physicians as human beings. They became our buddies, allies, and friends, creating connections among us that were very different from physician/nurse relationships back home. There the interactions were usually more of a servant/master. A handful of physicians were on the ship for the whole voyage but most physicians served for two months. Because of their brief stay, they depended on the nurses to orient and guide them through the quirks of the system. I overheard a physician talking to a new rotator as they made rounds one morning, "If you're smart, you'll listen to the nurses. They know what they're doing and can be a big help." Being a HOPE nurse was a heady experience that left me forever incapable of tolerating any patronizing or condescending physician behavior.

These relationships continued off duty, of course, and inevitable romances evolved. The nurses had to show each new group the ropes, including how to do their own laundry. They tried hard to bribe us into doing it for them, even saying they would buy us dinner on shore, but most of us wouldn't fall for it. We made them take us to dinner just for showing them how to *use* the washer and drier. The fact that I was an ex-Nun took them a while to process and they often quizzed me. One doctor had a motorcycle and would invite me to hop on the back while he did errands in the marketplace. Every time we came to a stop and could hear each other speak, he would have another question for me: What was the convent like? How did it feel to leave? I was getting better at answering these questions, but was still in the process of sorting things out. The questions helped me look at those eight years and be less glib than I had been when I first left.

True to our HOPE culture, we gave parties at the end of each two-month rotation. It was hard to say good-by and we covered up feelings of loss with humor. The permanent staff wrote goofy skits and the rotators retaliated with skits of their own. Our skit-writing committee would meet in one of the cabins and, fortified with a bottle of scotch and a huge jar of peanuts, wait for inspiration. We would get sidetracked with discussions about life and love and would have to plan another evening to write skits without the aid of scotch and peanuts. One of our skits was a take-off on *Snow White and the Seven Dwarfs* titled, "Dr. Monto and the Seven Dopey Nurses." Dr. Monto was one of the rotators who had given the impression he did not like nurses when he first arrived on board. We figured he needed a good razzing to remind him of how much he had changed. The skit turned out great and he loved it. After he returned to the States, we received a thank-you note from his nurses.

In addition to a skit, the rotators usually threw us a party. One group organized a farewell shindig in their dorm which they called *Chambachu* (The Jungle). It was a big room that looked like a patient ward. The party invitation read:

TO: HOPE Permanent North American Gringos and Gringas
FROM: HOPE Rotators
Your current crop of aging, semi-alcoholic rotators have unanimously agreed that The HOPE permanent staff has rendered them service well above and beyond the call of duty.
To show our appreciation, the rotating staff asks your presence at a party in The Jungle at 8:00 on the evening of Wednesday, June 7.
We would stress that this will be a dignified, quiet, intellectual evening which will make you remember some of your duller evenings in the U.S.A.
We plan to serve fruit punch in subdued surroundings. There will be poetry readings, a Bach string quartet, and a few edibles from Schrafts. Dress is informal.
Remember... the next group of rotators may be worse!

The party was anything but dull. The Jungle was noisy with party chatter and we spilled on to the deck for delicious food and a local band. I loved to dance to Latin music and grabbed rotators to be my dance partners, whether they wanted to or not. Each group of rotators was different and had their own group personality. We cried when they left and wondered what the next batch would be like.

As the months flew by, work on the ship did not become any easier. It became more challenging. Our patients seemed sicker. Some we kept on board for a long time to monitor their recovery after a complex surgery. One of the most memorable patients was a young man who had elephantiasis. He was a nice-looking kid, about nineteen and very personable. He had been with us almost from day one. Elephantiasis, a chronic infectious condition, is characterized by enlargement of skin and the tissue underneath to the point of severe deformity caused by the lymphatic vessels becoming blocked. During surgery, our plastic surgeons removed excess tissue and reconstructed the skin on his legs and scrotum. He needed a second major surgery to finish the process, plus some minor surgeries and skin grafts. After the operations, we considered him a miracle patient because he looked so different. He thought he was a miracle patient, also, when he realized his

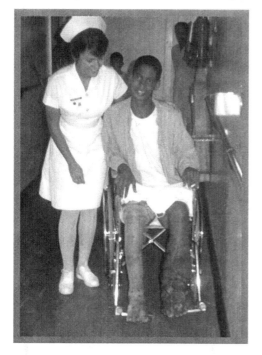

penis and scrotum would be functional. I cried when he finally left. Some of his positive energy lingered and the ward seemed empty without him.

I never quit looking for new experiences. Whenever I had some free time I would volunteer to help the nurses work in the *barrios* because I wanted to understand more about our patients' backgrounds. Several mornings I spent with our nutritionist, visiting the homes of malnourished children. Her job was to begin a teaching program for the mothers about what nutritional foods would be best to buy with their limited incomes. I became overwhelmed with the flies, the mud, and the sight of seven to ten people living in one small room. What struck me most was the look of total exhaustion on the faces of the mothers. One evening I accompanied our nutritionist while she showed a Walt Disney health movie in Spanish to a large group. Afterward, we were walking down the muddy strip that served as a road, and some children ran up to touch our hands and then stood staring at us. They liked us *gringas*. It was a humbling experience. I felt more valuable there than I ever felt in the convent.

At other times I volunteered to help our Public Health nurses implement an immunization program. Mostly I gave shots to children who waited in long lines. I would wipe an arm with a cotton ball in preparation for the shot and be amazed at the amount of dirt that came off. It dawned on me these children played outside in the dust and mud all the time because there were no paved playgrounds or streets for them to use. I quit trying to make their arms perfectly clean and gave the injection after one swipe. The work was hot, hard, and smelly, but I enjoyed interacting with the delightful children. Not one of them cried or resisted the injection. Clearly, they had been prepared to take whatever we would give them.

ꙮ

During those months of engrossing work, I had not totally forgotten about my own needs. I knew that losing my virginity was bound to happen sometime. I was twenty-eight years old, attractive, and ready. A nice guy came along who was more than willing to help me out. He didn't turn out to be Mr. Right or the

Love of My Life. But then, he didn't turn out to be a jerk, either. He was good-looking and intelligent and he liked me. He was a medical student helping out on the ship for the summer and we met at happy hour. How appropriate. His first impression of me was not favorable. "You looked way too wholesome!" Then he found out I'd been in a convent for eight years and decided I must have done a lot of thinking and might be worth talking to. And talk we did! He really listened to what I had to say. I was encouraged by his sincerity and told him things I had not told anyone before, not because I didn't want to tell but because no one else seemed genuinely interested. We swam, talked, ran, walked, talked, sat on the beach, and talked some more. We went to parties on the sun deck of the ship, danced to the music of the Mamas and Papas and talked till 3:00 A.M. many nights. One evening we sat out in the rain listening to "Madam Butterfly." He was a part of the new culture of openness and honesty. Sometimes he frightened me with his directness. I wasn't used to it. No subject was avoided, and if I became evasive he would call me on it. He helped me take a good look at myself and what I thought and felt, for which I was grateful.

He and I became part of a larger group of medical students and nurses who called themselves The Free Swingers, a totally innocent name at the time. The rotating chaplain was part of our group and would pass the word around the ship that there was to be a "prayer meeting" up on the sun deck about ten-ish. Then he would pass a "collection plate" for money to buy rum and Coke. One of the oft-repeated sayings of the group was, "We are constantly re-defining happiness." I knew I was doing just that.

The fun times with this special group only lasted a few weeks and then it was time for them to leave. After listening to my friend moan about waiting for *hours* for his connecting flight *alone* in the Barranquilla airport, I agreed to accompany him (airfare was all of $2.50). We sat together on the short flight from Cartagena to Barranquilla, and I had little doubt we would take the opportunity to go to bed together. We did. We rented a room at the hotel Del Prado, a lovely Spanish-style place with lots of atmosphere. I felt I knew what I was doing and I was also pretty sure I would never see him again. I cared about him as a friend and trusted him, but I had no need to hang on to him. I was tired of being a virgin. It was just the right time. FINALLY.

The sex was no big deal and happened very easily. I was amazed by my lack of guilt after all those years of conditioning. What I felt instead was relief. I kept thinking, "Wow! This is nice!" There was an embarrassing moment, though, when the maid walked in on us. I was totally flustered when it happened, but he and I laughed later, saying it would make a fun scene in a movie. After he left for the airport, I took the time to walk around the lovely hotel courtyard. I couldn't help but wonder if the maid who had walked in on us blabbed to every worker in the hotel, not realizing that she'd probably seen that a few times before!

I returned to the ship feeling like a different person. I even wondered if I looked different. I wasn't ready to talk about it so I kept to myself for a few days. I got my period a few days after that and felt a huge sense of relief. I had heard stories of women getting pregnant no matter what time of the month they had sex, and I had moments of panic at the thought. I hadn't evolved *that* far! Safe sex was not yet the big issue it would become in the 1980s. Safe sex mostly meant not getting pregnant.

‿

For weeks and weeks I considered what I wanted to do after the year in Cartagena. It felt like a hundred things went through my head, but only a handful of possibilities seemed interesting. One thought was to return on the next HOPE voyage to Ceylon (now called Sri Lanka), an island off the coast of India. It would expose me to a totally different culture from anything I had experienced. Or I could work in Europe. Mel had spent a year as a nurse in England and made it sound interesting. If my need for adventure evaporated, I could go back to school for a masters, probably in San Francisco. I didn't think I would go back to Omaha for any length of time. There were just too many other things I wanted to do and see.

I wrote long letters to my sister, Marty, telling her as much as I was capable of saying in a letter. Articulating my experiences and feelings was new for me. She was in college and busy dating. She sent me various pictures of herself, which several guys on the ship would yank right out of my hand saying, "She can write to me any time. Tell her my address is the same as yours!" They would race me to the mailboxes, pretending they were frantically looking for mail and photos from Marty.

There were about 600 Peace Corps volunteers in Colombia. Periodically, some would wander onto the ship looking for conversation in English, a drink, and a good meal. They were a nice group and gave the United States a good name. I had thought about joining the Peace Corps before going on HOPE but didn't want to be as isolated as they were. I didn't mind a *little* hardship, but I thought I had deprived myself long enough in the convent. Besides, Peace Corps people made even less money than HOPE people. One evening, five Peace Corps guys came to happy hour, so I rounded up four other nurses to go on a picnic with them. After stopping in the marketplace for roasted chickens, loaves of bread, and the eternal rum and Coke, we headed to the beach, where we built a fire, sang, and told stories. They were so grateful and so much fun! I ran into a few of them another evening when I was at a local nightclub named *Zorbas*. One of the Colombian men had his hands all over me on the dance floor and just in the nick of time, one of the Peace Corps guys cut in and rescued me. We danced for a while and then watched some of the liquor-saturated locals try to dance in a spotlight to the music from the movie *Zorba*. No amount of encouragement would get me out there with them. I did have my limits.

⌐

The Colombian head nurse I had been working with on the ship was ready to go back to her hospital on shore and start making changes. I spent the next month with her at Santa Clara helping her prioritize projects and implement what we could. She and the other nurses had difficult schedules. They were expected to be on duty twelve hours a day, five days a week. Most of the direct patient care medications, dressing changes, and starting an I.V. was done by auxiliaries who had about a fifth-grade education and one year of training. Many times there was no water, which meant they had no clean linen. Surgeries would have to be canceled for days because instruments could not be washed. When it rained, the water just drained away and no provision was made to save it for periods of drought. We tried to talk about methods for storing water but got reprimanded by the locals for worrying too much. To them, Americans did not have enough of the *manana* attitude. I couldn't begin to understand why nothing was being done about the water situation when water was so important to a hospital.

⌐

The heat, the smells, and the stress of constantly speaking in a foreign language were wearing on me. I could feel myself needing time off and was pleasantly surprised to hear we would get two weeks of vacation. Other staff members were planning and plotting which places in South America they absolutely had to see. I toyed with the idea of going back to Omaha for Barb's wedding, something I really did not want to miss. Then the invitation came for my brother Bruce's wedding a few weeks before Barbs', and I realized I could not go to one without going to the other. But two weeks was not enough vacation time to go to both! I also hated to miss an opportunity to see more of South America. I stewed. My three roommates invited me to join them when they went to Peru. I stewed some more.

With impeccable timing, a letter came from Patrick. He was helping set up a Jesuit University on the outskirts of Buenos Aires, Argentina, and invited me to visit. "I guarantee colorful tours with witty side comments, conversations with the natives, and the beautiful city of Buenos Aires, which, in my opinion, has few rivals." He and I had been friends for so long I knew I would have a fun time. He had a place for me to stay with an American and his wife. I knew that's what I wanted to do. Talk about a fork in the road. That decision changed my life for many years to come.

I borrowed some money from another nurse and was soon on a plane to Buenos Aires (with a stopover in Lima, Peru, to play tourist with some other Hopies). I was surprised that I felt nervous about seeing Patrick again. What would he think of this childhood friend of his? Why was I going all the way from one end of South America to the other to see him? Was this something I had to do before going on with my life? Was there any substance to the attraction I had always felt toward him? Would he continue with his plans to be ordained a Jesuit priest? I fantasized about us being the perfect couple with so much in common. I felt I could trust him. Trust was very important to me.

He was waiting for me at the airport. When I saw him, my heart did cartwheels. We hugged like long-lost friends and held hands as we chatted on the bus ride to the city. He looked wonderful. He was charming, tall, and attractive. His eyes were a beautiful blue. His voice was low and intimate, which made me feel I was the only person in his world. I inhaled his warmth and was aware of thinking during the bus ride, "I care for this man. He is a soul mate."

I stayed with his friends who had a lovely apartment overlooking a park in the heart of the city. The first evening I was there, the four of us went out for a Chinese dinner and then Patrick and I walked through the park alone. We talked about our childhoods, our parents, school, mutual friends, and, finally, our feelings about each other. He had incredible charm, which I later learned could be a dangerous thing. But, at the time, I totally trusted this person I considered almost family. We kissed, and I knew I had fallen irretrievably in love. I wanted to break out in song, but controlled myself and simply told him I loved him. Who knows why or how the heart falls so hard and so fast. When I was with him he was attentive, affectionate, and fun. He would hold my hand and tell me how soft it was; he would rub my arms and tell me how wonderful I was. How pathetically easy it was for him to charm me.

He would talk about us being married and what it would be like having me as his wife. No one had ever talked to me like that. I can remember thinking, "Someone who knows both Barb and me is actually falling in love with me instead of her!" Guys had always fallen head over heels for Barb and wouldn't even notice me. I had become accustomed to the sidekick role and it felt *fantastic* being the main attraction.

We didn't make love during that week. That came later in our relationship. Instead, we held each other and talked. I didn't question anything. I just went with my feelings. He introduced me to a beautiful student of his, and when he was busy at the university she would take me shopping and to her home. She and I developed a lasting friendship and years later I learned she was just as much in love with him as I was. He had encouraged her as he was encouraging me. When I could finally look back on those days with some objectivity, I was able to see clues that he was not being honest with me. But I was too much in love and too trusting to notice at the time. I didn't know I needed to be careful with him. My guard was not up like it had been in other dating situations.

⁓

As the week wore on Patrick became remote and distracted. I attributed his mood to a struggle regarding me. Me, me, me, I was the important one in his life. I didn't have a clue that he had other women on his mind, in addition to deciding on his future as a Jesuit. He was scheduled to be ordained a priest in three years which meant he could not marry. His friend with whom I was staying observed my feelings and said he had a long talk with Patrick. (I can only assume he encouraged him to be honest with me.) When Patrick and I were alone, he kept telling me he loved me very much, but he didn't know what to do. I thought he was just talking about being a Jesuit. I kept asking myself, "Why Patrick, of all the men I could have loved?" I had a terrible time saying good-bye. Leaving him at the airport felt as if I were leaving my life behind. He said nothing reassuring about what he was thinking. I spent the long flights home with an emptiness in the pit of my stomach, staring out the window of the plane wondering, "What now?" I was a goner.

Falling in love was one of the easiest things I have ever done.

Dealing with it was the most painful thing I have ever done. When I arrived back on the ship, I felt empty and confused, wondering why love hurt so much. I felt so alone. I struggled to find someone with whom to talk and confided in a friend who had also been with the Jesuits for several years. I thought he would understand and maybe have some sage advice. He wasn't a whole lot of help. His first comment was, "Wow, an ex-Nun. He's got good taste!" So I went to my room and wrote to Marty but even to her I could hardly put my feelings on paper. When I did start telling people about my vacation and Patrick, they couldn't quite figure out how I fell so hard in such a short time. To me, it wasn't that quick. I had spent years being drawn toward him. I soon learned he was a man of few words and I endured weeks and months with no letters from him.

I wrote to him frequently with the hope he would respond. The silence was terrible. I gave more thought about going on the voyage to Sri Lanka, but my hope was Patrick would leave the Jesuits and I'd be planning my wedding. Oh, how I wished for that! There was no way I could go back to Omaha and sit there waiting for him to decide. But was Sri Lanka the answer? It seemed so far away. Maybe, I thought, that would be good. If Patrick left the Jesuits, he would need some time to adjust without me. As it turned out, he would need more than time.

$$\backsim$$

Socializing became increasingly difficult because I didn't have the motivation. Mel pulled me out of my slump by involving me in another skit for the rotator show. We sat out on the deck with glasses of brandy and wrote lyrics. We did a take-off on the Peter, Paul, and Mary song, "Stewball," poking fun at a good-looking doctor. The nurses had been teasing him about being so handsome. He would become embarrassed so we razzed him some more. Mel and I performed the song wearing big red hearts pinned all over our clothes and acting as if we had big crushes on him. He laughed and then got more razzing.

~

Life on the ship settled into the everyday mundane and I settled in with it. I was starting to gain weight with all the good food around. I wasn't alone. The chef on the ship felt his contribution to Project HOPE was keeping the nurses well fed with things like homemade bread, steaks every Sunday, and yummy fried chicken. He would stand by the food line and watch to see how much each one of us was putting on our plates. When we worked the night shift and slept through a meal, he would save us food, whether we wanted it or not. He was able to buy fresh vegetables and fruits in the marketplace, but he became frustrated toward the end of the year when our frozen meat supply ran low. We kept telling him peanut butter sandwiches would do fine. Then, maybe we could diet!

I was spending part of my workdays on shore in the Santa Clara Hospital, which was both a wonderful and an exhausting experience. The rains finally came and almost flooded the place. The humidity made me long for the noisy air conditioning of the ship. I worked with another HOPE nurse who was setting up an intensive care unit, the first ICU in all of South America. Even in the U.S. an intensive care unit was a relatively new way to provide close monitoring to patients by nursing staff. Prior to this, the surgical death rate at Santa Clara had been high. Patients would be left in the hallway after surgery until a nurse happened by and would wheel him/her to the ward. It took us hours of work to ready the space, equipment, and staff. It took even more hours to ensure its function. We were so proud of that simple unit! And so were the Colombian nurses.

～

The smell of urine, infected wounds, and perspiring bodies is what got me the most when I worked in Santa Clara, and I had to fight nausea constantly. I didn't know how the Colombian nurses kept going. On the floor where I worked, there was one needle and one syringe for a ward of thirty to forty patients. Understatement: the needle was dull. In order to give an injection, a nurse would have to find out when the needle and syringe were being sterilized in boiling water (when there was water) and then hope she could get it for her patient. Frequently, injections could not be given in the necessary time frame or would be omitted altogether. It was heartbreaking to watch the nurses try to make sense out of their situation. To make matters worse, they would go for months without being paid.

The nurses also struggled with a lack of other equipment, like an EKG machine which was crucial in alerting staff about potential heart attacks. Much of their equipment had become rusted or lacked parts for repair. My job was to help my counterpart make what changes she could. She had wanted things to be different and more efficient for a long time but needed help overcoming the inertia of the other nurses. Sometimes we succeeded, sometimes we didn't. Having the Ship HOPE in the harbor at least gave the local staff the message that someone cared.

～

Toward the end of my time in South America, Patrick finally wrote. He hadn't made a decision about his vocation as a Jesuit but was touching base with me. He said he loved me. He said he missed me. He said the time we spent together was very special. As

I was reading the letter, my heart felt like it was leaping out of my chest. I didn't know if my tears were from sadness or joy. Both, I guess. It felt so good to hear from him! I fantasized about us being married, having children, and leading an interesting life of travel. I felt so sure he was The One. I did not want to listen to thoughts that even hinted he might not be right for me. The head and the heart don't always speak to each other.

The year was going quickly, and I needed to make a decision about going to Sri Lanka. It didn't look like Patrick was going to rescue me from traveling half way around the world and working my buns off again, so I committed to another voyage. A part of me knew the coming year was not going to be easy. Mostly, I blocked the thought. I did not hear from Patrick again for several months.

Wrapping up the year on The HOPE was a euphoric and depressing process for most of us. It was hard to think about leaving, but all of a sudden we were ready to go. During the last few weeks, new patients were no longer admitted to the ship so the census dropped each day, and the wards took on a strange emptiness. I felt like someone had pulled the plug and drained all my strength. So I smiled and was polite and kept telling myself it would be over soon.

I was running out of the basics I had brought with me, like shampoo, deodorant, and toothpaste. I tried a deodorant from the *Pharmacia* in the city, and it burned my armpits. I wasn't alone. Hopies would go from room to room on the ship saying things like, "I have some extra toothpaste, want to swap it for some deodorant?" Notes started appearing on the bulletin boards: DESPERATE. ANYONE HAVE EXTRA SHAMPOO? Tampons were impossible to find in the local drugstores so we had to use whatever pads were available. We all began appreciating drugstores back home. We were appreciating a lot of things: family, privacy, grocery stores, paved roads, beauty salons with hot water, and quiet air conditioning.

On departure day, Mel and I were up watching the sunrise. I knew my friends back home would not believe me, but I did see the sun come up without having been awake all night. There was excitement in the air. Several of our Colombian counterparts came on the ship to say good-bye. Some were crying. In the midst of all the confusion, many items of equipment were stolen. We figured the Colombians thought they needed it worse than we did, but it felt lousy to be ripped-off. We kept hoping, somehow, we'd made a significant impact on the health care in Colombia. I wondered how long the local nurses would continue to implement changes we had encouraged them to make. One of our recommendations was to keep sterilizing solution in the forceps jar at all times, something that took about six months to implement (with a lot of prodding). Would the birds' nests stay out of the local operating room? We were leaving a small group of Hopies behind, a Land Team that would stay for two years to increase the odds for the changes becoming permanent. I wished them a whole lot of luck.

We had been told the Colombians would not do a grand farewell since it's not customary for them to have big good-byes. Boy, was that information wrong! There was an estimated *twelve thousand* people shouting and waving at us. Some were on the docks and the streets, others out in the bay in small boats. One boy stood up in a canoe and waved a new crutch at us. As the ship moved out of the harbor, most of us stood in silence, leaning against the railing, watching the land get smaller in the distance. I realized that the emotions were overwhelming me. Too late. I fainted. Talk about "hitting the deck!" At least I had plenty of medical people around to help me.

On the two week voyage home, I was able to reflect on

how important it had been for me to be a part of something so significant. We had saved lives, taught/reinforced good medical practice, encouraged health care workers to continue in their struggle with incredible circumstances, and given the message that those of us who had more were willing to share. The voyage was a leisurely, luxuriously quiet time. I was up every morning wandering around the decks sipping on my coffee and watching the sunrises. We spent our days soaking up the last of the rays on the sun deck, still oblivious to the damage the sun could do to our skin. There were bodies lying all over catching up on sleep or working on a suntan to show off back home. In the midst of all those bikini-clad bodies was a three-year old Colombian child running around looking cute. He was accompanying us back to the states to be adopted by the sister of one of our nurses. He hadn't always been so cute. He had come on the ship several months earlier so weak he couldn't lift his head off the bed. He had surgery on a bad ear and was treated for malnutrition. His mother never came back to get him. It took him a long time to learn to smile and play, but learn he did and he became our wonder boy. So many times that year we would exhaust ourselves getting a child well enough to go home to the *barrios* and then see him/her re-admitted weeks later looking as bad or worse than the first time with a distended belly, skinny arms and legs, sad eyes and expressionless face. Our only consolation and hope was that, with all the teaching and changes happening in Cartagena, maybe some of the children would stay well.

Those of us who were coming back on the next voyage to Sri Lanka met with Dottie and discussed our needs. I let her know I wanted to work part of the time in the Kandy hospital, which was about a two-hour drive up-country from the port city of Colombo, where the ship would be docked. Our trunks were brought up from the hold so we could get ready and be ready for customs before we docked. Our room was a mess, but I no longer cared.

"What's the first thing you're going to do when we get back to the U.S.?"

"Kiss the ground."

"Eat real ice cream."

"Take several baths."

"Cry for joy."

＄

We arrived back in Philadelphia on December 16, 1967. The department store, Wannamakers, had a beautifully decorated Christmas tree lowered onto our helicopter deck as we sailed into the harbor. A band and hundreds of people were waiting to give us hugs and kisses. It was *cold*. Of course, there was a cocktail reception which made us feel like royalty again. I called Omaha to say hi. It was good to be back. For one thing, everyone spoke English! I enjoyed all the excitement the best I could, considering I was totally preoccupied with thoughts of Patrick. I knew I didn't want to give in to the feelings of grief and loneliness, but it took a tremendous effort to enjoy what I had. I was clinging to the belief that someone loved me.

⤳ SRI LANKA ⤳

(Ceylon)

I did *not* want to be someone who loved and lost, and I fought the thought. Fighting didn't help much. I spent the three months between voyages with my family, trying to act and be happy. It took everything I had not to dissolve into tears at the least provocation. I heard nothing from Patrick, not a thing. I wanted to turn the pain into anger but didn't know how. All I could do was keep going. There were very few self-help books, no Oprah on television, no counselors easily available. I didn't know where to turn for help. My parents loved me but were incapable of talking about feelings. Marty tried but could not comprehend what I had been through. Besides, she thought she was in love, and *he* worshiped the ground she walked on. Barb had married and moved to Phoenix. I went around mumbling our convent saying of, *Thank You God. Dang it.*

A local television station had filmed me arriving at the Omaha airport. While the whole family watched the 6:00 and 10:00 news, my brothers and I razzed each other: "I can't believe I hugged you in public!" I kept busy giving talks and showing my slides about HOPE. I was interviewed on television and featured in the magazine section of the Sunday paper. Life was fun as long as I didn't stop and feel.

⌐⌐

I worked in pediatrics at the hospital run by the Sisters of Mercy. I would hold little babies and wonder if I would ever have any of my own. The Sister who was the director of nursing helped me get some pediatric experience since I would be working pediatrics on the next voyage. She thought it was wonderful that I was on The HOPE. She also thought it would be great publicity for the hospital that a *LIFE* photographer was going to film me at work for a documentary about HOPE. I had met the photographer when he was on the ship in Cartagena. His plan was to show a HOPE nurse (me) at home and at work in her local hospital and then again on the ship in Sri Lanka. I was *so* excited I had been picked to be the nurse. I had just received a script with shooting dates when the whole project was canceled! I never did find out why. Funding, I think. I was bummed. Mom and Dad had been avid fans of *LIFE* magazine for as long as I could remember and were looking forward to the filming at home. I hated disappointing them. Life itself was getting a bit too disappointing for me. I had become accustomed to all the attention and envisioned a semi-celebrity status from being in a movie. However, I would have given up every single moment of it for Patrick. He felt so far away, physically and emotionally.

⌐⌐

Several of the Sisters of Mercy I had known organized a get-together with others who had left the convent in the last three years. I couldn't believe so many had left after I did! I had a great time catching up on their lives. The ones who were still in the convent were changing their lifestyle dramatically. They could go back to using their birth names and wearing an updated habit or contemporary clothes. Many of them were starting to live together in smaller groups, renting houses or apartments close to the hospitals and schools where they were working. They no longer had to go through the gut-wrenching appointments handed down from the Provincial Council every year. They simply asked for a particular job they wanted to do and then finances were worked out for a local budget. When I was in the convent, we never even *saw* money, let alone have control of it! The training of the new Sisters had also changed dramatically. There were only a handful of new recruits compared with the 100 in the novitiate when I entered. The ones who remained in the convent seemed much more relaxed, though not relaxed enough for me to wish I were one of them! I never did look back and wonder. I've always been glad I decided to leave.

I received sad news about Sister Robert Mary, the other Sister who was in nursing school with me. Evidently, she had been getting her hands on Demerol, a narcotic pain killer, when we were students. How she did that, I have no idea. In hindsight, I realized taking drugs must have been part of the reason for her mood swings. She left the convent, got caught stealing drugs on the job, lost her nursing license, drank heavily, and finally committed suicide by hanging. I could hardly comprehend it. I had known her so well but hardly knew her at all. In retrospect I wonder how I ever survived her. She had so many talents but must have been in chaotic emotional pain.

‟

March came quickly, and I was glad to arrive back on the ship. Mel and I were roommates again. This time, however, we had enough seniority to have a nicer two-person cabin. There was room to put things! Two Hopies from previous voyages were in the cabin next to us and we used their blender for creative drinks and their porthole to pass snacks outside for happy hour on deck. Parties started right away as we were getting unpacked. We hugged and kissed old friends and greeted the rookies. The closeness of The HOPE staff was comforting; I needed these friends. I also felt the need to be aware of how much I was drinking. Being the child of an alcoholic mother made me terrified of becoming dependent on alcohol and there was always plenty around. I resolved to limit myself to no more than two drinks per evening.

Departure day in Philadelphia was cold and raining. At least we didn't have a blizzard like the year before, and sailing was only one hour late. I had changed so much since the previous voyage. I didn't know if I was more mature or just older. I certainly was more realistic. I was glad to be there but didn't feel the thrill of the first voyage. When I stopped for any length of time I felt the pain of Patrick. I was fine with my decision to go on another voyage, I just couldn't control the ache in my psyche.

The 12,000 mile voyage to Sri Lanka would take six weeks. We stopped for publicity in Fort Lauderdale where some of us threatened Dr. Walsh with chartering a plane, knowing we had a long voyage ahead of us. He just laughed. We were half-serious. Three days on shore helped, though. We had an eye-popping reception in West Palm Beach at the mansion (Mar-A-Lago) of Marjorie Merriweather Post, a leading American socialite and founder of General Foods. I tasted my first fresh strawberries dipped in chocolate (flown in from her favorite deli in New York). I had to be dragged away from the table.

After Ft. Lauderdale, the sea gave us hours of rolling and pitching like I had never experienced before. Time blurred and frequently I had to ask what day it was. The turbulence left several people confined to their bunks with seasickness. One of the staff had to be airlifted back to the states because she could not stop vomiting. I felt almost guilty because I got my sea legs quickly and could eat and sleep.

Dottie was our director of nursing again. She had been on the advance team to Sri Lanka in between voyages, gathering information and planning how she would use her nurses. We spent much of the voyage in meetings with her getting updated on what she had learned. Two men from Sri Lanka sailed with us and shared wonderful information about the country and its customs. Every day for an hour, one of them, a pilot for Pan Am, did his best to teach us Singhalese, or Sinhala, the language of Sri Lanka. It would have taken us too long to master writing Singhalese so we settled for memorizing words phonetically. We learned to count to ten and sing the national anthem that started with, "Sri Lanka…." meaning beautiful country. Prior to 1948, it had been a colony of England so most of the adults were fluent in English. Singhalese had been declared their official language in 1956 and they quit teaching English in the schools at that time. Most of the population was Singhalese from northern India, and their religion was Buddhism. The second group, Tamils, were Hindus from southern India. They had been brought over to the island by the British to work the tea and rubber plantations and settled mostly in the northeastern part of the island. Several years after we left, a brutal civil war between those two groups tore the nation apart and killed thousands on both sides.

The days on the ship had become routine by the time we stopped for three hours to refuel in Trinidad. We dashed off the ship as fast as we could (considering we still felt wobbly from having sea legs), took a bus to San Fernando, and plopped on the beach. What a treat! We drank beer, swam in the beautiful water, and pretended we were on vacation. It was probably just as well we couldn't stay longer since we would have unwound so much our motivation would have suffered. As it was, mine was marginal as we headed back to the ship. I kept thinking about Patrick.

More storms hit us around the Cape of South Africa, but we persevered in our painting of the wards. The buckets didn't cooperate any better this time than they did on the way to Cartagena and I painted my nose more than once. We gradually became aware of how old and vulnerable the ship was. We would hover in the hallways staring at the ship's expansion belts as they creaked and groaned, hoping they would hold. I developed a backache bracing myself against the roll and pitch of the ship. The only time I enjoyed the waves was standing on the flying bridge about five stories above the water. Even then the waves were so high I'd get soaked to the skin but would hang on to the railing and enjoy every minute. Other times when the water was calm, I would watch the reflection of the moon or look over the railing where the ship cut the water, making the plankton show their florescence.

∽

A two-day stopover in Durban, South Africa, didn't come a moment too soon. We had not seen land for days and were almost desperate to go on shore. But once we heard that the rules of apartheid dictated we could not be seen with our black HOPE staff, we wanted to stay on the ship to show our disapproval. It took hours of diplomatic maneuvering from Dr. Walsh, the American Consul from Durban, and the black staff themselves, to bring us around. We grudgingly accepted the reminder that we were not representing ourselves individually and that the purpose of Project HOPE was to help, not to cause trouble. Dr. Walsh also pointed out we were guests in South Africa and this was no time to create a disturbance. We continued to feel unresolved but agreed to cooperate. The handful of black staff stayed on board while we departed, and then they went on shore. The irony of our struggle with racism in South Africa was the timing. We heard about the assassination of Martin Luther King while we were docked in Durban.

The fresh air in our hotel room was conducive to deep sleep after so many nights with the ship's noisy air conditioning. In the morning three other nurses and I pampered ourselves by ordering "bed tea" delivered to our room while we took turns soaking in the bathtub. We finally relaxed enough to explore Durban. The city struck us as very similar to Miami with its hotels and beaches. We did the usual touristy stuff of a bus ride to the game preserves of Natal's Lion Park to stare at the animals and take pictures with the Zulus.

Weeks of mail caught up with us while we were in Durban. Among several fun letters from Marty was one from Patrick. He hadn't made a final decision regarding the Jesuits but was seriously leaning toward leaving. He apologized for not writing, saying he needed time to think things through. He said he loved me. I wanted to talk to him so badly but I knew it would be a long time before I had that luxury. I was willing to wait if he was there at the end of the wait. Just hearing from him reinforced my feeling that I was not imagining our relationship. The letter put me in a wonderful mood. The slowness of international mail gave it a depth and power that is not found in today's communications.

～

The next leg of our voyage was peaceful. The weather was balmy so several of us dragged our mattresses out on deck at night. The stars were huge and the sound of the waves put us to sleep almost immediately. Sunrises were magnificent. If we awakened early enough, we could grab coffee and curl back up on the mattresses to enjoy the color and serenity. However, if we overslept, we were rudely awakened by the sound of crews heading our way hosing down the decks. I think they enjoyed startling us.

We arrived at Colombo, Sri Lanka, on April 16, 1968. It was hot and humid. The ceremonies at the Queen Elizabeth Quay went on and on with the prime minister, Mr. Dudley Senanayake, and many others welcoming us. We wowed the crowd with our singing of the national anthem which a local radio station taped and played over and over. As a local newspaper reported, "A chorus of twanging *Ayuboyans*[1] in American accents rang over the murky water in Colombo Harbor from the throats of nearly 200 angels (both sexes) of Mercy in immaculate white, leaning against the railings of the Hospital Ship HOPE as she steamed majestically to her berth." We thought the description was a bit dramatic, but nice. We would have welcomed dramatic-but-nice-later in the year when the political climate changed and the tone of newspaper articles became hostile. During all the arrangements of getting the ship to Sri Lanka, the government was pro-American. As we journeyed to the island, a surprising election changed the government to Communist. We were left with the resulting hostility, but the preexisting contracts committed them to work with us. It was like the wrong date showing up at the front door and the tension escalated the longer we were there.

◡

Colombo is the huge, sprawling capitol city on the island of Sri Lanka which is 270 miles long and about 25,000 miles square.

---

[1] *Ayubowan means "greetings" or "may your life be a long and happy one."*

The coast is desert but changes inland to an elevation of 8,000 feet with beautiful, green mountains, or "up country," where the tea plantations make use of the plentiful rainfall. The coastal beaches have white sand. Depending on the season, one side of the island has clear, blue water while the other side has cloudy, murky water. Every bit of the island is fascinating to explore.

⌒

In the midst of all the hustle and bustle of arriving, our precious mail was waiting. I took mine to my cabin, shut the door, sat down, and savored each one. Patrick's friend whom I had stayed with in Buenos Aires, wrote a wonderful, long letter. He said Patrick had decided to leave the Jesuits and was returning to the States. My first reaction to the letter was sheer joy that Patrick was becoming "available." My second thought was why wasn't Patrick the one to tell me? Again, I rode the emotional roller coaster of one moment feeling elated and the next feeling sad. Patrick was just outside my grasp of understanding, a characteristic of our relationship that never changed. But for a long, long time, I was unable to stop reaching.

I had learned over the years how to grin and bear it. After indulging in some tears, I took a deep breath, opened my cabin door, and faced the work ahead which would prove to be even more difficult than the previous voyage because of the political situation. We had come halfway around the world and didn't want to give up easily. A Russian ship sat across from us in the harbor; previously, it had been the U.S.S. Liberty from the Lend-Lease Program. The irony of it all was that the Russians never paid the United States for it. Now we were looking at it every day and facing hostility because of the influence of Communist Russia.

Anne aboard The Hope, 1968

The first group of HOPE staff to work up-country left for Kandy almost immediately. Of course, we had a party before they left and nicknamed them the Kandy Kids. Even though they would be only two hours away by car none of us wanted to say good-bye. We stayed out on deck after the party and watched a perfect sunset, listened to a recording of *The Messiah*, drank brandy, and, once again, began our philosophical discussions. By midnight we had solved all the problems of the world yet again.

Mel was one of the Kandy Kids, so I was without a roommate. That changed as soon as the rotating doctors arrived. Dr. Margaret Storkan, a dermatologist from California, bounced into my cabin looking like a perfect imitation of Miss Marple from the Agatha Christie books and movies. She was short, round, white-haired, and wore an impish grin. I wanted to hug her the minute I saw her. She talked nonstop, bobbing her head up and down, carried a little red purse, and wore practical, white Nun-like shoes on her tiny feet. She was just what I needed to dispel some of the heaviness in my heart, teaching me by example how to be joyful.

I was assigned to stay on board and work pediatrics, but joined the tours of local hospitals, knowing I would work on shore at some point. The pediatric hospital, Lady Ridgeway, consisted of several buildings connected by walkways with roofs but no walls. The hospital walls went up to eye level, while pillars held up the roof providing a flow of air when there *was* a flow of air. This design was the norm for the hospitals in Sri Lanka.

Our tour of Colombo General Hospital was even more impressive. They had several *floor patients* or *mat patients* who brought their own mats and slept on the floor when there were not enough beds. Most of the time there were about 1500 patients for 1000 beds. During the day, the floor patients would roll up their mats and roam around the hospital. I never did figure out how the nurses kept track of them. I think there was some unwritten code that told the patients when they needed to be available for medications and procedures.

Our evenings were busy with invitations to dinner at the homes of local physicians who were trying their best to welcome us in spite of the politics. I enjoyed being in their homes which were decorated with brilliant colors and fascinating designs. I did not enjoy eating curry on everything. The Sri Lankans made sure we knew which foods had baby curry and which had adult curry. The baby curry made my eyes water and my nose run so I stuck with that, unable to imagine what adult curry would do to me. Even the locals had to regress to baby curry if they had been out of the country for very long. I learned to eat with my fingers since people kept telling me, "The food tastes much better that way!" I gave it a try and wished I had a bib.

⌣

My first week in pediatrics was slow since we hadn't yet admitted very many patients to the ship. To keep busy I rode up country to Kandy in The HOPE van which was bringing supplies. I saw my first elephants up close. Our driver stopped so I could watch an elephant being bathed. As we sat in the van at the side of the road, the driver explained how deep the relationship is

Hospital Ship HOPE, 1968

between elephant and owner. "An elephant will work for one person, and one person only, who is called a *mahout*. It takes fifteen years to train an elephant. It will become cantankerous and refuse to work if not given a good bath and scraping with a coconut shell the day before." The rice fields were a lush green, speckled with people working in their sarongs and saris. Most of the locals seemed to know who we were and waved with great enthusiasm. Sri Lanka is called the teardrop of India because of its shape and proximity to the coast of India. Immigration from India had been discouraged for years. There was poverty on the island, but its natural resources provided the basics of food and work so it didn't have the overpopulation and depths of poverty that seemed to plague most of India.

We stayed for dinner with the Kandy Kids who were living at the Hotel Suisse which overlooked Kandy Lake. Even though the hotel had become run down over the years, it was more luxurious than I had expected. Lord Mountbatten had stayed there during World War II and one of his local servants was still at the hotel and served us dinner. He looked about sixty years old, was barefoot, and wore a sarong. He had a large smile underneath a long, white moustache curled with precision at the edges. He bowed and scraped like I had never seen before. "More to eat, Missy?" "You enjoy dinner, Missy?" Like most people from Sri Lanka, he had the mannerism of moving his head in a ball bearing motion instead of up and down or side to side. We Americans never really knew whether he was saying yes or no. When in a dilemma he would say, "Not knowing what to do, Missy, simply not knowing what to do."

⤳

Back on the ship, I worked days, and relished the slowness of the pace. I would take the children outside so they could enjoy the sunshine and view the city. As soon as they warmed up from being out of the air conditioning, they began playing and running around on deck. They made me laugh.

Our days were ruled by the local Poya calendar, which followed the cycles of the moon, so that a week could be anywhere from four to nine days. The week began with Poya Day, equivalent to our Sunday, then Poya 1, Poya 2, and so on, until the last day of the week, which was called Pre-Poya and was similar to our Saturday. We became a bit cross-eyed trying to figure out which day of the week it was on our calendar compared with theirs. Using the Poya calendar helped Sri Lanka promote their identity after so many years as a British Colony. The drawback was that the Poya calendar limited the number of days for trading with other countries since most holidays and weekends were different.

⤳

Toward the end of April, Marty wrote that Patrick had come to our house in Omaha for a visit. I was starting to get angry. Why was he not writing? Once again, why did I have to learn of these major events through someone other than Patrick? I looked for excuses, like a letter lost in the mail. Of course, I was thrilled he had actually left the Jesuits and pleased he had come to visit my family. I spread the word around the ship and pretty soon several of us were drinking champagne and toasting

Anne and Patrick. If my friends **had doubts** about how things were evolving, they kept them to **themselves**. A letter from Patrick arrived a few days later. The tone of his letter sounded vague and not very reassuring. He kept saying he **loved me** and missed me but his actions were confusing me. However, I took his words at face value and enjoyed the peace and **calmness** they brought me. I was so in love. All I could think about **was going** back to the States. When I signed up for the year, **I had no idea** Patrick would decide to act so quickly. The time was **starting to drag** already. The months ahead would become very long.

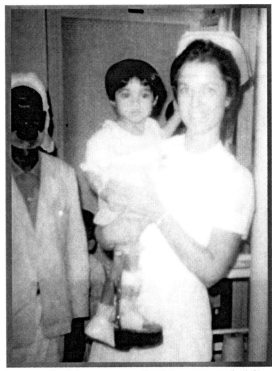

Anne holding Jainathul Umma, child's, grandfather in background 1968

I did the only thing I could and immersed myself in my work. Children of Sri Lanka are beautiful and gentle and one by one they stole pieces of my heart. A little three-year old girl, Jainathul Umma, had me thinking seriously about adopting. None of her family was visiting so I thought they had abandoned her. As a toddler, she had fallen into a fire used for cooking in the home. The burn on the back of her leg had received minimal treatment. As a result, the muscles had shriveled, bending her leg back so scar tissue attached the calf of her leg to her thigh. Until she came on the ship, she had hobbled on her good leg. One of our plastic surgeons operated on her, releasing the skin and tendons so her leg could straighten, and then applied skin grafts. Her foot was deformed and her burned leg was shorter, so she was given a brace with an elevated shoe enabling her to walk. Before she got her brace, I would take her to my cabin in the evenings, watching the amazement on her face as she continued to realize she could use her shorter leg. She would balance herself on the sofa cushions and hobble around. I grew to love her. Looking back, I realize I saw my sister, Mary Jo, in this child's sweet face and silent suffering. I wanted to take her back to the States and help her in ways I had not been able to help Mary Jo. Then, one afternoon, Jainathul Umma's dear grandfather arrived at the ward. I stood watching him hold her and tears rolled down my cheeks. The love in her eyes showed me she belonged with him. Later, I heard the family had not visited because they couldn't afford trips to the city. They saved enough for one person to go and decided grandpa, as her favorite, would be the most consolation to her. He was the first person to make her smile and her face lit up every time he walked through the door. I was glad for her but very sad that I was losing her.

⁀

Days off were filled with things to see and do. Dr. Margaret, my delightful roommate, usually invited me to join her in visiting the countryside with local friends. I called her the Unofficial Ambassador to Sri Lanka because she had made more friends in two weeks than most of us made the whole time we were there. We toured a tea plantation, a jewel mine, and a rubber factory. The tea plantation is what fascinated me the most; the women who picked tea were paid two and a half cents a day. I began to realize why some of them abandoned their newborns in the hospital. There was no way they could provide for them, especially with several others at home. The tea was so fresh and brewed so perfectly that I quickly became an avid tea drinker—but only of Sri Lankan tea. The man leading our tour stated, "We send the dregs of our tea to America for their tea bags." No wonder I had preferred coffee!

The jewel mine was more primitive than I had ever imagined. Since Sri Lanka had some of the largest mines in the world, I had envisioned us going down into a shaft with long tunnels. Instead, the mines consisted of trenches with men in loincloths sifting through mud with pans. We were told that whenever a star sapphire was found, everyone would stop working and celebrate. The rubber factory didn't thrill me at all, and I couldn't remember a thing about it once I left except that it had a terrible smell.

﹏

Dr. Margaret inadvertently arranged for one of my most memorable experiences of that year. Treatment of leprosy had become one of her specialties as a dermatologist, so the local doctors asked for her help at their leper colony. When she saw the place, she decided cleaning and painting were first on the list before she would be willing to deal with the medical challenges. She came back to the ship and did some heavy lobbying with the staff. First, she had to convince us that leprosy was not contagious on superficial contact and that much could be done for these patients with medication and surgery. Up to that point, most of us had outdated information from medical textbooks and the Bible. When we voiced concern about being around the disease, she said, "Poppycock! Double Poppycock!" as her head bobbed up and down. So off we went, this van loaded with "volunteers," heading into the unknown because we trusted her.

Normally, we would show up at a work facility in our traditional white uniforms, but that day our outfits looked more like items from the Goodwill reject pile. We wore headscarves, t-shirts, cut-offs, and tennis shoes. Dr. Margaret looked the grubbiest of us all. She had borrowed a pair of slacks that were way too long for her so the crotch hit her at the knees and the pant legs were rolled about ten times. She didn't care and neither did we, once we stopped laughing.

The leprosarium was in an isolated area of Hendola about seven miles outside of Colombo, and the ride in the truck took us through some run-down sections of the city, including the fish market. Seeing all the flies and smelling the stink made me wonder if I would ever eat fish again. As we rode down the narrow, winding roads, we sang the Sri Lankan National Anthem that we had learned on the voyage over. The singing helped reduce our anxiety and prompted one of the physicians to dub us Camp HOPE. The diversion worked, though, and we arrived humming, chattering, and oblivious to a group of men with leprosy, who had slowly migrated out of the buildings and were staring at us. They couldn't believe us. They had never had company before, let alone female company. (Dr. Margaret had only been there for a short assessment visit.) There were about 600 lepers and the females were separated from the males. The patients were further divided into groups by religions: Buddhist, Hindu, Muslim, and Christian. The living quarters had been badly neglected and wore an ugly gray color. The structures were similar to the other hospitals in Sri Lanka with the height of walls being about eye level and the roofs held up with pillars. We were told one seventy-year-old man had been in the leprosarium since he was seventeen. I couldn't imagine. Many of the patients did not even have leprosy, but because whatever they had *looked* like leprosy they were sent there just in case!

Dr. Margaret had informed the officials at the leprosarium she would provide the labor if they would provide the cleaning equipment and the paint, which they did with great enthusiasm. She had even convinced a couple of local nurses to join us, although they did not participate in our dress code and showed up in uniform. As casually as possible we set about our work slapping white paint on the walls. It was difficult for me not to stare at the lepers' disfigured faces, let alone not wince at the smelly, fly-ridden bandages. They watched us closely. Pretty soon they lost their shyness and, some one-handed or one-legged, helped us move furniture. They asked for our brushes and started painting, laughing and talking while we took our turn watching. I never thought I would see people with leprosy laughing. I never thought I would see people with leprosy.

When we brought out the cameras, the lepers competed to get into the pictures, which surprised me. I thought they would feel too self-conscious. Instead, they were enjoying the attention.

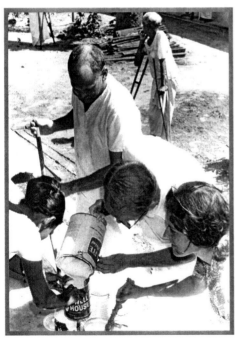

One of the pictures taken by The HOPE staff, my favorite, was of a Ceylonese nurse, two of the HOPE surgeons, and myself mixing paint in a huge Maxwell House coffee can. In the background was one of the lepers leaning on crutches watching us. It captured a moment of amazing acceptance, teamwork, and lack of pretension.

The afternoon was hot and humid, and we were less

than fragrant by the time we finished. As we stood around grinning and congratulating each other on a job well done, the lepers challenged us to a game of softball on a dirt lot nearby and we hesitantly accepted. They played amazingly well, considering their physical limitations. They certainly played better than I did. I fell into my old routine of tripping and giggling and they giggled along with me. One patient put his arm around me, and I didn't even feel a need to pull away. It would have been impossible for me to refuse such a genuine gesture. To show their gratitude, some of the patients cut open coconuts and offered us the milk which we drank and enjoyed. As we pulled away in the "Camp HOPE" truck, all of them were standing on the road, waving. We were much quieter on our return trip to Colombo, each one of us with our own thoughts.

Back on the ship, I became even more immersed in my work with the children. I enjoyed the week on nights and waking the younger ones to prepare them for the day. They would laugh and play and give hugs. The only part of early morning I dreaded was changing diapers. The children were given medicine for worms before they went to sleep at night, so changing their diapers the next morning was a challenge. I never adapted to seeing worms in their diapers and had to fight back the nausea each time I saw them. The children and I communicated easily, most of it with sign language since I knew only a few Singhalese words, like *tikak polowa* (glass of water) or *balana* (look). I gradually added *kohomoda*, (how are you?), *atta*, (true) or *boru* (not true). Amazingly, the children understood English words if we put *–eka* at the end, as in, "Get in the bed-eka." We Hopies found ourselves talking to each other that way, "Are you going to the party-eka?"

I visited Kandy frequently. It was such a peaceful place compared to the noise of the ship and the city of Colombo. There were several abandoned children in the pediatric ward who had never set foot outside the cement floors of the Kandy hospital. They had worn hospital gowns their whole lives, had no toys, and had grown up around sick children. The Sri Lankan nurses seemed to accept them as a fact of life, but The HOPE nurses could not. They went to work getting the children immunized, treated for lice, and placed in an orphanage where they had a chance of being adopted.

Several of us Hopies took five of these children to a park for an afternoon where they could experience the feel of grass under their bare feet. A couple of them wiped out a bed of flowers before we could rein in their enthusiasm for smelling and touching. They ran in all directions and found a pond for splashing. I had never seen such joy. The ride to and from the park was not as much fun for them since the feel and sound of The HOPE van was so unfamiliar. They sat on our laps, too frightened of the rushing scenery to let go. I held one child close to me and hoped the gentian violet we used for treating lice was doing its job on his little shaved head. He was so scared he was trembling. Later, unable to put him out of my mind, I wrote a poem:

KIRI BANDA
I held a child today,
Gently.
His head was covered with
"Live creatures,"
His ears with scabs.
His hands were swollen
And his bottom bare.
But I loved him as if
He were the cleanest child
I had ever known.

I held this child
Who clung to me
Out of fear.
We were exploring his new world
Together,
Riding in the "van-eka."
And slowly,
As fear slipped away,
His muscles no longer
Clung to me.
He looked when I said,
"Balana."
He smiled when we saw
An elephant.
His first.
We sat in the grass
Together
Eating chocolate
Learning to touch the earth.
And when
Our lesson was over,
We stopped.
Again, we must return
To the confines of a hospital.
But he had touched life
A little more
He had known joy.
And I held him closely.

In spite of my efforts to stay motivated, I floundered professionally, emotionally, and physically during this time. Morale was low on the ship as the government of Sri Lanka continued to resist the presence of Project HOPE. The staff kept busy, but we constantly dealt with the undercurrent of not being wanted. Several articles had come out in the papers with questions like: Why is the U.S. in the Vietnam War? Are they trying to kill all Asians? Are they prolonging the war so they can kill all their blacks who are the ones doing the fighting? Dr. Walsh was threatening to pull the ship out of Sri Lanka and go where we could accomplish more. It was hard to be optimistic, knowing the many negative things that were being murmured behind our backs. More articles appeared in the local papers, questioning the qualifications of the American doctors because anyone who had not been educated in England was suspect. The articles accused us of experimenting with the locals and posing as a hospital while actually being an electronic spy ship. They even accused the doctors and nurses of playing strip poker. We had been asked to come and then were being treated as if we had invaded them and attacked their professionalism. We were getting tired of it all.

In addition, we were hearing overwhelming news from the States. Senator Kennedy had been shot while he was running for President. He cared about people who were left on the outside looking in, the same population we served. We talked in small groups. What was becoming of the country we had left behind? The chaos with student demonstrations, anger over Viet Nam, and riots and burnings in Washington were hard to imagine. We knew we would have even bigger adjustments to make when we returned home. We had left during the beginnings of change. Now, from a distance, we could see the political, social, and sexual changes escalating. I had only just begun to adjust to life outside the convent, let alone to the radical changes of life in the United States.

Patrick was, of course, another reason for my floundering. I wanted to scream with frustration because weeks that seemed like months would go by without a letter. I told myself that if he would write to tell me he didn't love me any more, it would be easier than not hearing at all. I would have understood his needing time and space to adjust to life outside the seminary, but I had no patience with silence. He was telling me how he felt by not writing, but I could not hear his message. I felt so helpless. I wrote to him every once in a while and wondered what he thought when he read my letters. My friends on the ship could not believe how he was treating me. Neither could I. One of the hard parts about being so preoccupied with Patrick was I had no motivation or energy to pursue other relationships with men who came into my life. I couldn't even pretend I was interested.

I was physically floundering from working extra hours. Some of the nurses were sick with Dengue Fever which caused aching muscles and fever and made them look like they had measles. We were all vulnerable to catching Dengue Fever since it was transmitted through flies; our fatigue made us even more susceptible.

Touring the beautiful island of Sri Lanka became an effective diversion for many of us when we did have time off. The loveliest place for me was a resort in Trincomalee, or Trinco, as we came to call it. The Tourist Center House sat on a cliff overlooking the ocean. It saddens me now to think it was washed away by the Tsunami of 2004. But then it was beautiful and quiet with only the sound of the waves hitting the rocks. Those of us with the same long week-ends off would spend hours scuba diving, walking the beach, and writing long letters home.

To cross the island from Colombo to Trinco, we took a cab, a risky venture since the drivers played "chicken," swerving to miss each other at the last second. They enjoyed throwing us into a panic. We begged our driver to slow down (*Hemen yanna! Hemmen yanna!*), which only made him more daring. Before starting out on the trip to Trinco, we had flipped a coin to see who would be the lucky one to ride the suicide seat in front. I lost the toss and spent most of the ride with my eyes shut, my favorite way of avoiding scary stuff. When we arrived safely at our destination, we thanked the grinning driver profusely (*"Bohoma stuti"*) as we bolted from the vehicle. As dangerous as the cabs were, the old double-decker buses from England were worse. The bus drivers acted as if they were behind the wheel of a sports car and would swerve around country roads at breakneck speed, causing terrible accidents when they tipped over.

Days on the ship became routine. I volunteered again, this time to give other Hopies gamma globulin injections, a routine we went through every two months to protect against hepatitis. We also took Aralen pills for prevention of malaria. Out of eleven million people in Sri Lanka, two million had malaria, so the risk of getting it was great. Wednesday was Aralen Day with bowls of pills sitting on the table to remind us.

Dinner conversations often buzzed with the latest interesting event to see, fire walking being one of them. I didn't want to miss it, so I rolled my body out of bed in the middle of the night to join a group going to a ceremony in Kalonnewa, a village just outside the city. When we arrived, I hovered at the edge of the crowd, too amazed to get closer. Before the actual fire walking began, the participants had spent hours dancing to drums. All ages participated, some as young as ten. One of our physicians was so interested in the physiology of what happens, he took biopsies of participants' feet before and after the ceremony. Later, when he examined the samples under a microscope, he found no changes in the skin, even though the temperature of the coals was about 1000 degrees Fahrenheit and the participants had walked over the coals several times. I moved closer to see whether I could tell if they had worked themselves into a trance or had been drugged. I couldn't. They danced to honor the Hindu God of Kataragama. Other participants were putting hooks into the skin on their backs and dragging carts by these hooks. There was no moaning, no groaning. I had to look away again. I went back to the ship with my head full of images I did not want to remember. I mulled over how we humans have such a need for a god-figure, someone we can talk to and trust with our simple emotions and needs. I knew greater minds than mine spent years trying to make sense of it all, and I only hoped my experiences in life would clarify some of my thoughts.

⤳

Suddenly it was June and Dr. Margaret's two-month rotation was over. The Rotators' Show was especially difficult for me since it meant saying good-bye to her. By then, I knew every one of her mannerisms so I mimicked her in a skit that, I must say, was very funny. I put a mop on my head for her white hair, "borrowed" one of her dresses and a purse, and shoved my feet into a pair of her tiny shoes. About halfway through the skit, I began to have empathy for Cinderella's ugly stepsisters squeezing into the glass slipper! I could hardly keep a straight face as I bobbed my head up and down saying, "Poppycock! Double Poppycock!" Dr. Margaret loved the skit. A few days later, when she left for the airport, she gave me a lovely star sapphire ring as a going away present.

⤳

Some of the local doctors rose above the politics that surrounded us and kept inviting us to dinners in their homes. Usually, the evenings would be fun with interesting conversations about the history and future of Sri Lanka. The country had stopped importing goods and was unable to keep up with their production needs. Since they had no way to make cars, their cars and buses were old and constantly in need of repair and parts. A black market had developed for many items such as cotton, radios, and apples. I had been offered ten dollars for a partly used can of hair spray, a lot of money for what probably cost me less than two dollars. I just gave it to the nurse who wanted it.

Astrology was an important part of life in Sri Lanka and horoscopes were consulted for marriages and other important events. Many of us had our individual horoscopes done, not wanting to pass up an opportunity with the experts. Mine predicted a big change for me in November. "You will be leaving the country permanently. It's a good time for marriage." I interpreted that as a prediction I would be going back to the States soon. I was *hoping* that was what it meant.

So I asked Dottie about the possibility of going home before my contract was up. I had been mulling over the idea for weeks, not knowing what was the right thing to do. She gently suggested I would be better off staying for my own personal accomplishment. She said I was scheduled to work in Kandy for a couple of months and felt I would enjoy that. I was ambivalent. I was trying to make a mature decision, which was not easy to do since I was so emotional and *in love*. I felt if I could just see Patrick and talk with him, I could get my bearings about how serious this relationship really was. I was not objective enough to realize he was trying to tell me. I tried talking myself into staying with HOPE the whole year, and then had flashbacks about trying to stay in the convent because I thought I *should*. Not a good concept for me. If I stayed, I needed to *want* to be there.

By July, I was driving myself crazy with stay/go self-talk. I was working nights which gave me several hours of think time. I couldn't get Patrick off my mind. One morning, after finishing a particularly slow night in pediatrics, I walked on the beach for a couple of hours mulling over what to do. I finally went to the nearby Hotel Tapprobane and placed a call to him. I had to wait four hours for it to go through. When he finally did come on the line, the connection was clear as a bell but my mind had become muddled. My heart started beating so rapidly I could hardly talk.

The call wasn't consoling or clarifying. I didn't hear, "I love you and miss you," which was what I had hoped to hear. He sounded reluctant to ask me to come home. "I don't want you to be sorry that you gave up your wonderful opportunity to be on The HOPE." I couldn't tell if that was really the reason or if he did not want me there. He kept asking, "Are you all right?" I kept answering, "I guess so." I wasn't all right but I couldn't think of how to tell him I was miserable being so far away. I sensed he did not want to hear it. We finally agreed I would come home after my stay in Kandy. Or was that my decision? He had an uncanny ability to talk without saying anything. I hung up the phone more confused than before the call. I felt torn. "Well, Fangman," I mumbled, "stay for Kandy and then go home." I don't know why I kept struggling, why I couldn't hear the message he was sending me, that he was not that into me. I couldn't let go of The hope of a love of a lifetime.

During this time of decision-making, I tended to keep to myself. I didn't want to talk about Patrick. I knew my friends were worried. One of the physicians actually wrote to Patrick—and got an immediate reply! Patrick wrote him saying he was confused and wanted me to make my own decision. What *I* wanted to do was throw something and listen to it shatter all over the place. I wanted to yell at Patrick, "TALK TO ME!" Instead, I carried on as if I were in complete control. I fooled no one. I finally forced myself to do some socializing and met a couple of very nice British fellows who worked on the island. I hit it off with one of them but couldn't respond to his interest. I think I let another good guy go.

∽

I moved up to Kandy at the end of July. It was lovely to hear the sound of birds in the Temple Tree outside my bedroom window at the Hotel Suisse. I was now one of the Kandy Kids and the job felt rather daunting. My area of responsibility was a large surgical ward for women and children. Once again, the hospital was huge with hundreds of mat patients. It was located on a hill and each building was connected by the traditional long walkways

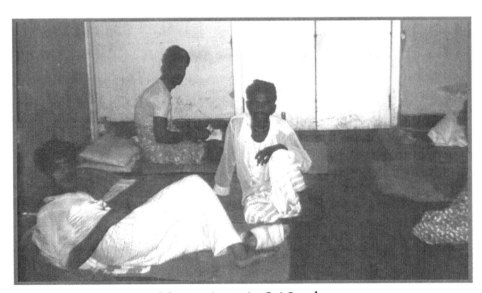

Mat patients in Sri Lanka

with roofs but no walls. During the monsoon season, the rain blew into the hospital areas and walking between buildings was a soggy experience. The openness of the wards allowed crows to fly into the wards and snatch food from children. It also let in flies, iguanas, lizards, and other creatures I didn't want to think about.

I immersed myself in work and tried to shut down my emotions. That helped for a while until I was faced with the sudden death of one of our high school volunteers from the States. She had been helping with projects while her father worked on the ship as a physician. She caught a staphylococcal infection that would not respond to treatment and spent several days in intensive care on the ship, struggling for survival. They did everything they could for her on the ship, and her death brought an anguish that was almost palpable when we called from Kandy. We felt helpless being so far away. Here we were, saving lives every day and we couldn't do anything for this dear girl. I had met her only briefly but felt overwhelmingly sad that one of us could get so sick and die. Several memorial ceremonies were held in Colombo and a Requiem High Mass was said for her in Kandy. It was the first time I had been to Mass in a long time and was comforted by attending something to express my grief for her family.

I rolled up my sleeves and went back to work. It felt good to be busy and challenged. There were certainly enough patients who needed attention! As an outcome of The Sri Lankan version of socialized medicine, adopted from the British, many patients were hospitalized for relatively insignificant conditions. It was difficult to get them to go home when they were well enough. Why go home when they had free food in the hospital? A big downside of their system was the inability of the government to pay for adequate staff, buildings, and equipment. Many doctors and dentists resorted to driving cabs while patients were left unattended in hospitals and clinics. The physicians who were lucky enough to be hired quickly became overwhelmed with the heavy workload.

The nurses didn't fare much better. The caste system prevailed, so most doctors ignored what the nurses had to say because they were from a lower socioeconomic level. Nurses also had difficult schedules, working all morning, leaving for a few hours in the afternoon when activity slowed, and then coming back in the evening. Housing was provided for them near the hospital. Since they worked for the government, they could be transferred anywhere on the island even if they had family who could not follow them. Their morale was low.

I spent a few days with the local head nurse of the ward, and we mulled over what to tackle first. My impression was that the place needed cleaning. Should we start with that? Would we need to have a follow-up cleaning schedule? Would that be condescending to the nurses? Or did we need to start with getting medications labeled? The head nurse decided she wanted to work on a system of accountability for post-operative patients. Up to that point, there was no recovery room so patients came back to the ward directly from surgery. One of the other HOPE nurses was organizing a recovery room/intensive care unit so she and I decided post-operative nursing care would become a priority for both of our wards. I spent much of my time encouraging the nurses to notice the surgery schedule, make assignments, and accept responsibility for patients as they came out of surgery. The nurses seemed enthusiastic when we discussed the subject, but then nothing was done unless the head nurse or I was right there directing traffic. I learned very quickly that changing behaviors is a tough job.

The local nurses thought we Americans tried too hard to interfere with the flow of life and death. We respected their

Buddhist beliefs but would get frustrated with the passivity they promoted. We would do CPR if the situation warranted, but none of the local nurses would participate and stood around watching us. Some of their reluctance to intervene was also due to the lack of functioning equipment to support them so they felt it was a losing battle to try, and I had to admit they had a point.

The laundry for the hospital was washed by hand and left on bushes to dry. During monsoon season, the sheets could not dry, so patients often slept on the protective rubber sheets that covered every mattress. The families of patients stayed to do care and feeding and they were polite and grateful for anything the nursing staff did.

I made cleaning of the utility room a priority since it was so dirty and so disorganized that no one could find anything, even items they desperately needed. For days I tried every motivation technique I knew, but all I got back was, "Yes, Missy." I finally started the process myself. Once things started looking better, the nurses began suggesting where they wanted equipment kept. The physician in charge of the ward promised he would get the pantry painted, but his request for paint became bogged down in government red tape.

Bugs and I were at odds. I began ridding the pantry of leftover food to discourage huge cockroaches. I couldn't stand the idea of all those bugs in the same room with patient food. This time when I went looking for help, I got, "Missy, the bugs come back." So I devised a plan:

"If I get bug spray from the ship and clean everything out, would you follow a daily cleaning program set up by your head nurse?"

"Yes, Missy."

"OK, let's tackle the patient areas first; I see families putting food in nightstands and some large bugs are in there." I acted braver than I felt when I took the nightstands out on the balcony and sprayed away. My activity drew quite a crowd to watch the *hundreds* of bugs pour out of each nightstand. It was gross. I jumped up on a chair. I tried to act in control, but the look on my face must have given me away. The audience laughed and clapped. I've often wondered how long those nightstands remained clean.

Nurses in Sri Lanka did not empty bedpans. Someone from a lower class was hired to do that chore. The bathrooms were neglected, and I fought nausea every time I even walked near them. I interacted with the "bedpan crew" because the nurses felt it was beneath them to have anything to do with the subject. Again, I talked about the importance of getting and keeping the bathrooms clean. The bathroom crew would use their ball bearing head motion, but they at least did what I asked. I did some of the scrubbing myself, which confused everyone because they thought the American nurses were near the top of the hierarchy. Afterward, the nurses had me soak my hands and arms in a caustic disinfectant. Then we posted a weekly cleaning schedule.

I began to notice confusion about passing medications. Pills were kept in five different places on the ward, making it difficult to find the correct ones. Also, the medications came in a wooden box from the pharmacy, each partition in the box containing a different medication. No labels. Also, there were no lids and the high humidity caused pills to glob together. The nurses were expected to recognize the pill and, hopefully, pull out the right dosage and give it to the right patient. I bargained, saying I would provide medicine bottles from the ship, label them, and put the correct medicines in the bottles if they would focus on reading each label before giving the medication and would put the lids back on the bottles. "Yes, Missy." I put hours of work into doing just that and even more hours gently reminding the nurses to put lids back on the bottles.

We kept hearing rumors that the workers on night shift slept most of the night. Three of us HOPE nurses decided to work a night shift. We wanted to see for ourselves what patient care was like on nights. Rumors were correct. Intravenous feedings ran dry and even the very sick patients were not checked. Wandering through the semi-dark buildings, we saw much more than we had bargained for, including snakes. Rats walked around as if they owned the place, while mat patients slept on the floors seemingly oblivious to their surroundings. The three of us were too spooked to leave each others' sight and stuck together like glue while we checked our wards. One night was enough. We didn't need to see more. Each one of us shared some of the information with the local charge nurse on days, but had little hope she could make any changes. She had enough of a challenge making changes on days.

When the rains came again, a couple of us got grumpy and decided we didn't want to socialize over dinner in the hotel dining area. We hibernated in our room, made tuna sandwiches from cans pilfered from the ship, and drank Chevas Regal scotch, which hit the spot! I think we could have written a song with catchy lyrics about tuna and scotch on a rainy night in Kandy.

Big Daddy Walsh visited Kandy to give a talk about the shaky status of the programs in Colombo. The main reason Kandy was successful was because the schools of medicine and dentistry were fairly new and not burdened with politics. Our relationships with the local doctors and dentists were pleasant.

⌣

I was lucky to be in Kandy for the Parahara. It is an annual festival honoring Buddha with several days of parades that included lavishly decorated elephants and the famous Kandyan dancers. Most of the dancers sported red teeth from chewing beetle nut leaves, a favorite activity of males in Sri Lanka; although the beetle nut has a tranquilizing effect when chewed, it also causes cancer of the throat and mouth. The culmination of the festival was a specially chosen elephant carrying Buddha's tooth from the Temple of the Tooth.

Several of the staff from the ship came up to Kandy to see parts of the Parahara. They crashed on our hotel room floors for the night since there was nowhere else to stay. Every hotel in the area was crammed with visitors who came from all over the world to see the celebration. The parades were like nothing I had ever seen before. Each night the participants tried to out-do each other with increasingly outrageous decoration on their elephants. It looked like something out of a movie with miles of dancers, elephants, acrobats, torchbearers, drummers, and musicians.

Naturally, the tourist trade was strong, and several enterprising locals made their elephants available for rides. I couldn't pass up the opportunity. Elephants are huge and it's a long way looking down from the top with only a flimsy rope for stability. My elephant was trained to kneel so his foot could be used as a step stool. I was told to grab the rope around his neck and shimmy to a sitting position behind his ears, not a very graceful procedure the way I did it. The handler gave me fruits and vegetables to feed the elephant. When that big trunk came toward me demanding a treat, I wasn't about to hesitate. One banana comin' up!

As if the festivities in Kandy were not enough, about ten of us (men and women) formed what we nicknamed the Schmirnoff Group. When we took pictures, we posed as if we were in a Schmirnoff vodka ad (popular at the time): our bodies draped across furniture or a car or some other prop, our cheeks

sucked in to look elegantly thin, and our heads thrown back to look down our noses. Sometimes we couldn't control our laughter long enough to get a decent picture. The Schmirnoff Group spent a weekend up-country in Nuwara Eliya at the Hill Club that used to be a favorite rest house for the British. It reflected the elegance of that era with a fireplace in each room and huge, overstuffed chairs. The servants stayed out of sight most of the time, but they knew exactly when we were heading up to our rooms and would scurry ahead to prepare the bed, start a fire, and put a hot water bottle under the covers. What service. They had been well trained by the British. I could have learned to live like that! I knew there was a big difference between how we Hopies lived and the way the locals lived, but I needed the break from the reality of it all.

On the Saturday of our weekend we set out to go horseback riding, but the deluge of rain stopped us. So we headed to the bar at the Hill Club and started drinking Bloody Marys. The day turned out to be very relaxing with a lot of laughter. I even smoked a whole pack of cigarettes, amazing for me since I didn't smoke. After I nurtured a couple of drinks, the gang challenged me to recite Prinderella and the Cince which I had learned while in the convent. Fooled them. I did it perfectly.

Late afternoon we broke up the party to grab naps and I woke up feeling less than charming. I was taking a very long time to dress for dinner so one of our group came up to my room to check on me. "You'll feel better if you put on more jewelry and brush your teeth again, Fangman." Pretty soon, someone else came up to check on me and said the same thing. By the time I arrived downstairs, I had on every piece of jewelry I could find and very clean teeth.

A few weeks later, the Schmirnoff group went to Hiddadurwa which is nine miles south of Colombo on the coast. We had two days of beautiful beaches, snorkeling, and swimming. On the train ride back there were no seats available inside, so I sat on my suitcase on the steps between the cars. It was a lucky inconvenience because the scenery was exquisite with graceful palms, sparkling ocean, primitive shacks, and a beautiful sunset. It was a lovely time for thinking. I tried not to think serious thoughts but they came to mind, anyway. I had run out of motivation for being in Sri Lanka even though the place remained lovely and the work challenging. I felt very done.

Back in Kandy I tried to re-motivate myself and continued to implement some changes on the ward. I didn't like the way I was feeling, but no self-talk would perk me up. Patrick had not written as he promised during our phone conversation. Well, my decision to go back to the States had been made and I was not about to change my mind at this stage. I was more than ready to face reality, whatever that reality turned out to be. I wrapped things up as well as I could and oriented The HOPE nurse who would be taking my place. I rode back to Colombo on the train with my local counterpart and her husband who were going to visit the ship. Since they couldn't afford first class tickets, I traveled with them in third class where passengers let their animals roam the cars. The crowding and smells were more than I was in the mood to handle.

It felt good to be back on the ship. My friends kept asking me how I was doing. They were worried about me, and I under-stood why. If I had known how they could have helped me, I would have asked. I went to the Embassy to sign off on paperwork and to the bank to get travelers' checks. Friends organized a happy hour and dinner on the sun deck in my honor. They gave me a lovely sterling silver platter with elephants around the edge and their names engraved in the center which I still have and cherish.

I cried. I hated leaving these people who were so good to me. I hoped with all my heart I was doing the right thing.

～ EPILOGUE ～

I arrived at Dulles International outside of Washington, D.C., very tired from my emotional departure from HOPE and the long trip. I could tell Patrick was distracted when he greeted me. I was so glad to be with him, I tried not to attach meaning to his mood. I stayed at a cousin's house in Virginia and he was in Georgetown. We spent time together; but he was frequently busy, and I often had to fend for myself. He would call, we would go out, we would talk but hardly ever communicate. When we had sex it was not that good but I was grateful for any physical contact. We both flew back (on different days) to Omaha for Christmas. Again, I hardly saw him, but when I did, he talked as if we were getting married and we could honeymoon in Ireland. I kept hanging on to the hope he meant what he said and told my family and friends. Looking back, I'm amazed that I was still willing to consider marriage and a honeymoon with a person who would hardly talk to me. I had grown up in a family that did not share feelings so didn't realize what was missing. I loved him and the thought of letting go was way too painful for me to face. After the holidays, we drove back to D.C. in my red Chevy (pried once again from the arms of my sister). Most of the trip was spent in silence. It was as if he weren't there, and I was unable to alter the emotional distance between us. I felt left out of his thoughts. At the time, I had no idea his preoccupation was other women.

I decided to work at Georgetown University Hospital and found a room to rent in a nearby townhouse. Even though I was physically closer, I saw even less of him during that time. In fact, he frequently stood me up and would not answer my phone calls. I remember driving in Georgetown listening to Simon and Garfunkel's *Parsley, Sage, Rosemary and Thyme* and thought my heart would break right then and there. I kept reaching out for him, but couldn't find anything to hold onto. I've had to consider seriously what that longing really meant. Was I trying to fill the hole that a distant and distracted Mother left in my psyche? Was I trying to fill the gaps left from a difficult childhood? Was I trying to make up for eight years in a convent? I still don't have all the answers. It's possible I never will.

Gradually, I began to learn about other women Patrick was involved with. Some of them were very serious about him. One day at lunch in the Georgetown Hospital cafeteria, I sat next to a female doctor who innocently told me about this wonderful man she was dating. She talked about his working at Georgetown University and how they were going away that week-end. I tried to keep my expression blank, but the realization that she was talking about Patrick made that very difficult. My heart was racing. Before I could put my thoughts together, let alone say anything, she got paged and left the table. I sat there in shock for a while and then had to rustle up enough of my convent discipline to go back to work.

The one time Patrick and I did have a serious discussion about our relationship, I said it was obvious he needed to sow some wild oats before settling down with me. He neither agreed nor disagreed but mumbled something about my not being able to handle the situation. He was right, in the sense I couldn't get angry and tell him to go to hell. I called home and cried on the phone telling my Dad how awful I felt. He suggested I come back to Omaha for another visit. During that visit I had a disturbing phone call from Patrick's Mother who berated me. "You're giving up on him too soon. If you really loved him, you would stick by him." She had recently met a woman he was dating and was not at all happy about her. I wanted to give her an earful of just exactly what her dear Patrick was capable of doing, but of course I didn't.

A few months later, back in D.C., I heard he was married (not to the doctor and not to the woman his Mother had met). He didn't have the courtesy to tell me himself; I heard it through the good old grapevine. I understood then how a person could die of a broken heart. My sense of trust was crushed. I had convinced myself I knew who he was because of our similar backgrounds, but I hadn't a clue. Mr. Right turned out to be so very wrong. Over the next several years, I would hear about him through mutual friends. His being married hadn't changed his behavior. He continued to break womens' hearts.

I had nowhere to go, no one who would talk to me other than to say, "You're better off without him." "Just forget about him; there will be someone else." I knew in my head they were right, but my heart had not even begun to agree. I struggled to overcome the deep feeling that I would never fall in love again. As I learned in the convent, I just had to grin and bear it. Healing comes slowly under those conditions.

I did not hear from Patrick until fourteen years later. We were both in Omaha attending our high school reunions. He had heard I was in town and called the home of the friend where I was staying. I was leaving that afternoon but he wanted to see me so we arranged to meet in Arizona where I was living. When we finally met for lunch, I was able to ask what the hell happened, and to tell him how hurt I had been. I still didn't get a response that made sense, only a comment that he had "really cared." Sounding sincere was his specialty. During our fairly long conversation, he casually mentioned some of the women he had been involved with over the years. In the next breath, he talked about his wife and children. I was appalled and, by then, very glad I had not been the chosen one. Undoubtedly, I would have wound up a single mother.

⌐

Crazy Barb and I have stayed in touch. We've not been as close as we were in high school and in the convent. We couldn't be. She married and raised three children. I went off into the life of the single person. Our third musketeer from high school, Dee, entered the convent the year after Barb and I did and is still a Sister of Mercy. The three of us have had reunions celebrating the fact that we reached the ripe old ages of sixty-five, seventy, and seventy-five, and were still functioning. We've laughed, drank wine, told stories on each other, looked at old photos and agreed we were pretty cool kids.

As for Braniff International Airlines, the company did great until deregulation brought bankruptcy in 1982. For a few years, a very conservative Braniff tried to carry on, but it never worked again. The zip was gone. I have remained grateful I had that brief, fun time working for them. It was just what I needed to loosen some of the constrictions I felt from convent life.

Project HOPE no longer has a ship. Finding large enough port cities that were politically stable and wanted/needed the

Ship HOPE became too difficult. The ship was scrapped in 1974. Since no one had ever served on the Ship with the background I had (convent and airlines), I realized I would be the only person who could ever claim that history. Project HOPE continues with several land-based programs all over the world doing wonderful work promoting Health Opportunities to People Everywhere.

Over the years, I continued to date, but tended to attract men who were not right for me. At least I didn't try to talk myself into marrying them. I think men made more of me than I was, putting me on a pedestal for one reason or another. I don't think they looked to see who I really was, who I had struggled to become. Most of them tried to control me, so I would end the relationship. Eventually, I realized that I needed my personal freedom more than I wanted or needed to be married.

I had highs and lows professionally, also. As jobs go, some were great and some were awful. I went to graduate school and earned a Masters in Interpersonal Communications, then took a nursing administrative job. That was not a fit. So I did some more teaching, which I have always loved. Over the years, I've tried on various professional hats: real estate, consulting, and modeling. I've found them all interesting but difficult to establish as a career while I was already busy earning a living. Nursing became my anchor. I've made the usual lifetime of mistakes and moving on when I could.

In the 1980s, I finally found a wonderful therapist in Seattle. She guided me through the maze of my family dynamics, my behavior as an adult child of an alcoholic, and my obsession with Patrick. Therapy was incredibly clarifying. It was like putting the right key in a lock. The rest of my life has been about turning the key and opening the door. Gradually, I've realized my long-term search was to replace the mothering I did not get as a child.

I tried Mother Church, Mother Stanislaus, Mother Provincial and the mothering profession of nursing. All they did was make me keep looking. Patrick mimicked Mom's behaviors of seeming to love me, but not being there for me emotionally and, in the long run, not there for me at all. His behavior was so familiar I thought it was love. I thank God every day that at least I had love from Dad who showed me what unconditional love felt like.

Since leaving the convent I've developed a clarity between religion and spirituality. I spent serious energy sorting out how I felt about both and realized I wanted to be spiritual but I didn't want anything further to do with organized religion. I'd had enough. Religion can make a person feel righteous and I look back with embarrassment at some of the rigidity I professed so adamantly. Religion also tended to block my quest for spirituality. Is there a God? I don't struggle with that question. For me, there is. My definition of God is a constant presence in me and in everyone and everything else. I'm usually content to live in the present, whether the present is pleasant or not.

Another question I've asked myself over the years is: am I sorry I even entered the convent? For a while after I left, I had to work through the anger phase of having missed so much "prime time." In my forties and fifties, I began to look at what those years had done for me. I can't imagine myself without that experience. Had I not entered, I might not have known who I am as clearly as I do now. I may not have had the discipline to attain goals or the inner strength to live my life peacefully no matter what else was happening. I still get angry, scared, frustrated, exhausted and confused, but my inner self remains safe. I have finally come to love myself as I am. I appreciate being able to breathe, smell, hear, touch, and love.

My dads' statement that I was "saved for something special" stayed with me, but my definition changed. Finding out who I really am, not who others *think* I am has been what has made me special. Those formative years becoming an adult gave me the strength I needed for the years ahead.

ACKNOWLEDGMENTS

Of course I don't know where to start, or where to end for that matter. Here I go: To every single person who encouraged me, especially co-workers. Numerous times I heard, "What an interesting life you've led!" "When can I read it?"

Specifically, I thank (not necessarily in order of importance): the late Erma Bombeck, the guys at Weiss Guys Car Wash in Phoenix, Bob Kaye, Elayne Puzan, Julie Bliss Umbriet, Cathie Haynes, Marty McKelvey, Barb Bundgaard, Tina Howard, Karl Urseth, Lynn Bryant, RoseMary Gray, Sister Mary Claudette, RSM (Dee), Jane Navone, Hadlock Computer Services, and many others who plowed through various versions of the manuscript.

ABOUT THE AUTHOR

Anne Fangman is a mystery to most people. She is a world traveler who started out in conservative Omaha, Nebraska. At age eighteen, she entered a convent where she stayed, reluctantly, for eight years. Finally figuring out she was the only one who could be responsible for her life, she left a month before final vows.

To balance out her life experience, Anne joined Braniff International as an airline stewardess and became the self-professed, "only twenty-seven-year-old-virgin airline stewardess in the history of flying." She then decided to use her nursing education and volunteered to go on the Hospital Ship HOPE, one voyage to Cartagena, Colombia and another to Sri Lanka.

After falling in love with her childhood crush who was, at the time, a Jesuit seminarian, she experienced the rude awakening that he was someone she could not trust, let alone marry. Realizing a broken heart needed time to mend, she kept her life interesting by getting a Masters in Interpersonal Communication, traveling broadly, becoming a model, working in the field of nursing, and optimistically dating (without much luck).

Anne now lives contentedly in the Seattle area with her Scottie, Lady MacBeth, and Westie, Sir MacDuff, who keep her somewhat under control.

CPSIA information can be obtained
at www.ICGtesting.com
Printed in the USA
FFOW03n0843070216
21239FF